SIR HALLEY STEWART TRUST: LECTURES

Volume 4

IS WAR OBSOLETE?

IS WAR OBSOLETE?

A Study of the Conflicting Claims of Religion and Citizenship

CHARLES E. RAVEN

Routledge
Taylor & Francis Group
LONDON AND NEW YORK

First published in 1935 by George Allen & Unwin Ltd.

This edition first published in 2025
by Routledge
4 Park Square, Milton Park, Abingdon, Oxon OX14 4RN

and by Routledge
605 Third Avenue, New York, NY 10158

Routledge is an imprint of the Taylor & Francis Group, an informa business

© 1935 Sir Halley Stewart Trust

All rights reserved. No part of this book may be reprinted or reproduced or utilised in any form or by any electronic, mechanical, or other means, now known or hereafter invented, including photocopying and recording, or in any information storage or retrieval system, without permission in writing from the publishers.

Trademark notice: Product or corporate names may be trademarks or registered trademarks, and are used only for identification and explanation without intent to infringe.

British Library Cataloguing in Publication Data
A catalogue record for this book is available from the British Library

ISBN: 978-1-032-88942-9 (Set)
ISBN: 978-1-032-87877-5 (Volume 4) (hbk)
ISBN: 978-1-032-87881-2 (Volume 4) (pbk)
ISBN: 978-1-003-53515-7 (Volume 4) (ebk)

DOI: 10.4324/9781003535157

Publisher's Note
The publisher has gone to great lengths to ensure the quality of this reprint but points out that some imperfections in the original copies may be apparent.

Disclaimer
The publisher has made every effort to trace copyright holders and would welcome correspondence from those they have been unable to trace.

This book is a re-issue originally published in 1935. The language used and views portrayed are a reflection of its era and no offence is meant by the Publishers to any reader by this re-publication.

THE
SIR HALLEY STEWART TRUST

FOUNDED 15TH DECEMBER 1924
FOR RESEARCH TOWARDS THE CHRISTIAN IDEAL IN ALL
SOCIAL LIFE

TRUSTEES:

SIR HALLEY STEWART, J.P., *President*.
PERCY MALCOLM STEWART, O.B.E., J.P., *Vice-President*.
BERNARD HALLEY STEWART, M.A., M.D., *Treasurer*.
SIR PERCY ALDEN, M.A., *Chairman*.
SIDNEY MALCOLM BERRY, M.A., D.D.
THOMAS HYWEL HUGHES, M.A., D.LIT., D.D.
ALBERT PEEL, M.A., D.LIT.
HAROLD BEAUMONT SHEPHEARD, M.A.
STANLEY UNWIN.

The objects of the Trust are *in general*:

To advance religion; to advance education; to relieve poverty; to promote other Charitable purposes beneficial to the community, and *in particular*:

1. To assist in the discovery of the best means by which "the mind of Christ" may be applied to extending the Kingdom of God by the prevention and removal of human misery;
2. To assist in the study of our Lord's life and teaching in their explicit and implicit application to the social relationships of man;
3. To express the mind of Christ in the realization of the Kingdom of God upon earth and in a national and a world-wide brotherhood;

For example:

For every Individual, by furthering such favourable opportunities of education, service, and leisure as shall enable him or her most perfectly to develop the body, mind, and spirit:

In all Social Life, whether domestic, industrial, or national, by securing a just environment, and

In International Relationships, by fostering good will between all races, tribes, peoples, and nations so as to secure the fulfilment of the hope of "peace on earth":

4. To provide fees for a Lecture or Lectures annually and prizes for essays or other written compositions, and to pay for their publication and distribution;
5. To provide, maintain, and assist Lectures and Research work in Social, Economic, Psychological, Medical, Surgical, or Educational subjects;
6. To make grants to Libraries;
7. To assist publications exclusively connected with the objects of the Trust (not being newspapers or exclusively denominational);
8. To make grants to and co-operate with Societies, Organizations, and Persons engaged in the furtherance of Charitable objects similar to the objects of the Trust;
9. To use the foregoing and any such other methods, whether of a like nature or not, as are lawful and reasonable and appropriate for the furtherance of the objects of the Trust.

The income of the Trust may not be used for dogmatic theological or ecclesiastical purposes other than the cult of the Science of God as manifest in man in the Son of Man in the person and teaching of Our Lord, "The Word of God," Who "liveth and abideth forever."

HALLEY STEWART LECTURE, 1934

IS WAR OBSOLETE?
*A Study of the Conflicting Claims of
Religion and Citizenship*

by
CHARLES E. RAVEN, D.D.
*Regius Professor of Divinity in the
University of Cambridge*

LONDON
GEORGE ALLEN & UNWIN LTD
MUSEUM STREET

FIRST PUBLISHED IN 1935

All rights reserved
PRINTED IN GREAT BRITAIN BY
UNWIN BROTHERS LTD., WOKING

TO THE MEMORY OF

EDWARD PARKER WALLMAN WEDD

AND OF ALL THOSE WHO WITH HIM
HAVE GIVEN THEIR LIVES
IN THE WAR TO END WAR

Thou shalt not build a house for my name because thou hast been a man of war and hast shed blood.

1 CHRONICLES xxviii. 3

NOTE

IF those who heard these lectures delivered fail to recognize them in their published form, it may be well to state that I have here followed my usual practice of lecturing without manuscript upon a theme already committed to paper. In these days the difference between the spoken and the written word is so great as almost to necessitate such a procedure. Lectures if read are generally difficult to follow; and speeches printed verbatim are still more generally unpleasant to read. Moreover, in this case the substance of the later lectures demanded fuller treatment than could have been given in a fifty-minute discourse. I have, however, tried to keep a popular style and to avoid technicalities and an apparatus of references.

C. E. R.

ELY
November 1934

CONTENTS

CHAPTER		PAGE
I.	INTRODUCTORY: THE SCOPE AND IMPORTANCE OF THE SUBJECT	17
II.	THE CONFLICT OF LOYALTIES	49
III.	THE PROBLEM OF GUIDANCE	71
IV.	THE CHRISTIAN AND THE STATE	93
V.	THE CHRISTIAN AND THE USE OF FORCE	125
VI.	THE CHRISTIAN AND THE ALTERNATIVE TO WAR	155
	INDEX	185

IS WAR OBSOLETE?

CHAPTER I

INTRODUCTORY: THE SCOPE AND IMPORTANCE OF THE SUBJECT

I

ON a Monday morning in September 1931, when the crisis of the previous month had shaken the foundations of our confidence, an invitation came to me to lunch that day in the Liverpool Cotton Exchange. My host, partner in a firm of international bankers, Colonel of Artillery in the war, a pillar of Church and State, put a note of urgency into his request. He had a question to ask: would I come and try to answer it? In his office he confronted me with it. "Here is the position," he said. "We are within sight of a complete breakdown of the whole structure of credit. If we get a National Government we may delay it for a few years. Even so, unless there is a radical change in the financial system, in industrial organization, and in world-politics, I see no hope of security. I've heard you talking about the Kingdom of God. Do you mean anything by it? Is it (forgive me) just hot air or has it any relevance to the present situation? I want to test that by asking you point-blank what a man in my position ought to do here and now."

Such questioning in these years of bewilderment will no doubt seem trivial. But in fact, and to our loss, it is not often that hard-headed men of affairs challenge their clergy to come down from the mountains of mist or vision and confront the epilepsy of the world. During luncheon we discussed some of the more obvious needs—currency reform, the lowering or abolition of tariffs, international labour agreements, the foundation of a world-wide commonwealth—the sort of problems which all of us were considering in those critical weeks. By them we reached his question. Manifestly such issues could not be settled on a purely British basis: the world was not yet ready for concerted action: while the threat of war darkened counsel, the nations could not gain the necessary confidence. Only if a first decisive step towards world-wide co-operation could be taken was there a chance that mankind would recover courage and the power to control its destiny. The Disarmament Conference had been planned: the nations had signed the Kellogg Pact. Here was a field, far simpler than currencies or tariffs, on which the vast majority were agreed. "Throw yourself heart and soul into the cause of peace: make sure that our country gives a clear and fearless lead for disarmament"—my answer could be nothing else.

Despite the long tale of disappointments during the past three years the conviction remains with me that the implementing of our pledges against war must be the first step to world order. No doubt the pull of ancient habit is still strong; vested interests and scare headlines complicate the issue; nationalism has been vastly strengthened and embittered by the events of the past decade: but beneath all this there is in the hearts of multitudes of simple and inarticulate folk a conscious hatred of war, a confused desire for peace, which no statesman has yet dared to recognize, but which an effective lead would surely call into action. At least it seems certain that if we cannot reach agreement here where the case is so strong and the alternative so intolerable, it is futile to expect a solution of the other great problems of international life.

But my luncheon was not to end so easily. My host was in complete agreement as to the need for peace. He could not resist the final remark, "How can you expect the representatives of the Powers to agree when you Christians—Romans, Anglicans, and Free Churchmen—cannot even unite to confer?" The memory of his last question is largely responsible for the present enquiry.

It is not for me to argue the necessity for peace, still less to discuss the political problems to be solved or the methods to be adopted for its establishment. Dr. Gilbert Murray, in the Halley Stewart Lectures for 1928, has surveyed the whole field with a cogency and charm, a knowledge and experience, to which I can make no claim. His great theme is altogether too high for me. Where the best minds of Western civilization are devoting themselves to the task, it would be the merest presumption for one whose work gives him no special qualification to attempt to follow their road. My purpose is far less comprehensive. It is simply to examine the peculiar responsibility of Christians in this matter, to reconsider the basis of Christian Pacifism, and to appeal to my fellows in the Churches to make up their minds on the issue and to act upon their decisions. The point of approach will be rather that of the individual than of the community, and of religion and ethics more than politics or philosophy. Much of the present perplexity arises in relation to questions which only the statesman and the expert are competent to decide. But their difficulties are enormously increased by the lack of any clear public opinion, by the conflict between ancient habit and half-conscious ideal in the minds of us all, and by the hesitancy of those who claim to possess a gospel of peace for mankind. The duty of working for peace rests to-day upon every thinking citizen: to no other cause is mankind more solemnly pledged. But a peculiar obligation rests upon the churches; their failure to respond to it cannot but be regarded as a betrayal of their essential claim; in the eyes of dispassionate observers it is probably the heaviest count in the indictment now being generally brought against institutional religion.

II

Christians who refuse to recognize the strength of that indictment would do well to read once more the last chapter in Mr. Graham Wallas's book *Our Social Heritage*. Writing in 1921 he sets out calmly and with a wealth of quotation the reply which he is bound to make to the Lambeth Appeal "to all men and women of good will." As one particularly addressed because "beyond the frontiers of the Christian Society," he examines the conduct of the Churches and especially of the Church of England during the years of war, criticizes both their response to the crisis and the validity of their prospects for the future, and decides that since sacramental emotion seems to be the dominant interest of Anglicans and since "its main defect as a basis for religion is its want of connection with any general ethical scheme," the only possible answer is that he must look to education to "hand on to boys and girls the heritage of a world-outlook deeper and wider and more helpful than that of modern Christendom." For a Christian such a chapter is a sobering and in places a tragic warning against easy indulgence in self-justifying optimism.

It may indeed be argued that Mr. Wallas relies upon evidence which few Christians would accept as representative, that the columns of the *Church Times* and the war-time utterances of the less intelligent Bishops are a travesty of Christianity, and that sacramental emotion in the sense which he imputes to it neither is nor ever has been the main-spring of discipleship in the reformed Churches. Moreover, in the years that separate us from 1921 the best efforts of these Churches have been devoted towards the recovery of a wider world outlook; the Conferences at Stockholm, Lausanne, and Jerusalem reveal unexpected resources and new grounds for hope; and in the particular question of war a great change has in fact taken place. But if such arguments justify a refusal to condemn institutional Christianity as entirely out of date, it must be admitted that its contribution to international peace is still woefully inadequate, and that unless a far more decisive agreement can be reached we cannot be confident that the Churches as at present constituted have any strong claim to consideration.

That there has been a great change in the outlook of Christians can hardly be disputed. Considering the extraordinary violence of passion during the war and in the disgraceful election of 1918 it was surprising to many of us that Christian pacifism and the conscientious objector met with so little recrimination. Almost before the ink of its signatures was dry, the Treaty of Versailles had ceased to commend itself: for a year or so those of us who denounced it as vindictive and unchristian found ourselves liable to interruption, but not for long. At the C.O.P.E.C. meeting at Birmingham in 1924, though the Committee hesitated about the possibility of including the question of war in its programme, not only was the Report definitely pacifist in tone, but a resolution that "all war is contrary to the spirit and teaching of Jesus Christ"* was carried after full and on the whole generous dis-

* *Proceedings*, pp. 172–9 and 287.

SCOPE AND IMPORTANCE OF THE SUBJECT 23

cussion. That the Conference laid itself open to attack by this decision testified to the fact that the Churches were not yet ready to endorse it: but when a similar clause that "war as a method of settling international disputes is incompatible with the teaching and example of our Lord Jesus Christ"[*] was passed unanimously by the Lambeth Conference in 1930, no one expressed either disapproval or surprise.

Those who were in close touch with Christian opinion will, I think, agree that the growing influence of pacifist views first became clearly marked at the tenth anniversary of the Armistice. Until 1928 it needed some courage to denounce war from a public platform, and with the exception of the Society of Friends no Christian Church had expressed any strong sense of its devotion to peace. That autumn saw a definite change. Since then not only have movements for the renunciation of war been established in the Congregational and Methodist denominations, but the atmosphere, which had previously become tense if any criticism of the legitimacy of war was expressed, now shows signs of resenting any attempt to justify it. The Christ and Peace Campaign in the following year organized united meetings in many of the chief towns and a concluding Conference at Oxford. The Church Committee of the League of Nations Union became active. The No More War Movement and the Fellowship of Reconciliation increased the measure

[*] *Report*, p. 46.

of their influence. Demonstrations and public meetings were organized by many local committees and Churches. In the autumn of 1931 the World Alliance held a notable Conference at Cambridge. In the spring of 1932 the proposal was made by a letter to the Press from Dr. Sheppard, Dr. Herbert Gray, and Dr. Maude Royden to enrol a Peace Army. On the surface it would appear that a far-reaching movement was sweeping the Churches into an enthusiasm for pacifism.

In view of such evidence it might perhaps be assumed that Christians had made up their minds upon the principles involved in the choice between war and peace; that they were prepared to endorse the findings of C.O.P.E.C. or of the Lambeth Conference; that Christianity had become identical with pacifism. If that were the case, the present enquiry would be unnecessary. Unfortunately, in spite of the increased influence of the cause and of the conversion to pacifism of a small number of prominent Churchmen, it is obvious that in fact there has been very little effort to think out the issue since the preparation of the C.O.P.E.C. report. Christians are still generally perplexed as to their duty; and their interest in peace is due less to clearer convictions than to the circumstances of the time.

It is to changes in the general situation that the wave of feeling against war owes its driving force. The final disappointment of the naïve belief in "a war to end war"; the increasing hardship accentuated by unemployment, monetary crises, political insecurity, and the failure of international conferences to achieve practical results; the stripping off of the last rags of glamour from war by a series of lurid novels, some of them powerfully realistic, others crudely pornographic; the outbreak of war in the Far East, the increasing tension in Europe, and the sudden success of the Nazi movement in Germany; these causes, while they played upon the fears of mankind and in certain quarters gave rise to demands for larger armaments, undoubtedly forced the Churches to realize that even a victorious war had failed to achieve its supposed benefits and that unless protests were made another outbreak of the same delusive madness might plunge civilization into ruin. There can be little doubt that at present the strength of the desire for peace does not indicate that Christians have examined the bearing of their faith upon the problem or that their enthusiasm has behind it a large weight of conscientious resolve.

If it be true that at present the motives of disillusionment, depression, disgust, and fear are mainly responsible for the increase of pacifism, then the situation is one which no Christian, however ardently he longs for peace, can regard with satisfaction.

Christianity despite the sneers of Nietzsche and the fatal caution of bishops, can never accept the creed of "safety first," or seek peace as a means to material prosperity, or renounce the zest and romance of living dangerously. War is so great an evil, war in the modern world would be so devastating, that to say that a peace of inertia, of self-preservation, of cowardice would be worse than war, might be an exaggeration. But plainly if mankind is going to surmount the difficulties and realize the opportunities of the new age, it will require a devotion, a self-sacrifice, and a courage as great as any militarist could demand. It is because the cause of Christian pacifism rightly understood is utterly opposed to any self-centred motives, and because without such understanding the peace movement may bring discredit on its supporters and disaster upon the souls of men, that the subject demands close attention.

III

The importance of the study of the problems has, of course, been repeatedly emphasized. We shall consider it in subsequent chapters under three heads —the conflict of loyalties, the element of struggle in the creative process, and the moral equivalent of war. But before doing so it is necessary to emphasize briefly the special importance and significance of the subject and to comment upon the reasons which make its discussion difficult.

The Christian is, after all, not primarily concerned with questions of expediency. He professes an allegiance to truth and righteousness for their own sakes and not as means to his own comfort or success. It is not enough for him to argue that war involves untold suffering or even that war would mean the ruin of civilization: earnestly as he must strive to allay pain, deeply as he must value culture and security, these cannot be his first concern. He claims to order his life in accordance not with the dictates of human prudence, but with the will of God as embodied in the life and example of Jesus Christ. He claims to seek no personal nor national nor universal advantage but God's Kingdom, in which alone all true values can be realized. As such, he must examine this matter of warfare in the light not of his own fears or desires but of his faith and knowledge, in the Spirit, so far as he can understand it, of his Master, and by applying to the circumstances of to-day the principles which that Master expresses and reveals.

To arrive at these principles might seem at first sight a simple task. The New Testament gives us not only a series of vivid pictures illustrating the attitude of Jesus towards His contemporaries and interpreting to us His mind and character, but a variety of other writings which show how His different disciples understood and acted upon His teaching. Widely as scholars still disagree in their rendering of the evidence, the main features of His character stand out with clearness and consistency. So plain is the resulting impression that a theologian so experienced as the Bishop of Gloucester[*] does not hesitate to sum up his exposition of the Christian life by urging that the Christian can best determine his conduct if he asks himself what Christ would have done under these circumstances. If a learned

[*] *What it Means to be a Christian*, p. 151.

and cautious bishop thinks it easy for simple folk to apply the example of Jesus to their daily doings, it would seem obvious that on an issue so direct as that of peace or war the Church could decide by bare reference to Scripture.

Yet Dr. Headlam, in spite of this advice, shows that, at least in this particular case, it does not lead to an immediate and unanimous verdict. In the previous paragraph he discusses the Christian's attitude to war, and not only asserts the "duty of giving up life if a man's country is attacked," but assumes almost dogmatically that warfare is inevitable and legitimate. To most of his readers it will seem a paradox if not a flat contradiction that a vindication of militarism and an exhortation to the imitation of Christ should stand side by side on the same page. At least it proves that the art of discipleship can be interpreted in startlingly different ways. Christians without exception will agree that their Master's example as set out in the New Testament is normative and that Christian ethics must be consistent with the records of Him: but to say so is not to suggest that He gave or intended to give a code of legal regulations that can be followed blindly or applied by rule of thumb.

It is indeed very noticeable both that every revival of Christianity has been in some sense a return to the historic Jesus, and that such return has always to be accompanied by a warning that His example must be followed in the spirit and not in the letter. Recent events have illustrated this double task. We have seen in the present century a very marked concentration of interest upon the earthly life of Jesus; Liberal Protestants and eschatologists, scholars and teachers, Free Churchmen and Anglicans, men of letters and men of affairs, have given us studies of His ministry, teaching, and influence. In consequence it has been necessary for others to emphasize not less definitely their conviction that for the solution of the problems of to-day it is not enough to rely upon a few selected texts or even to imitate literally the Master's actions: the art of living cannot be reduced to a mechanical obedience nor can the circumstances of the first century be treated as identical with those of the twentieth: there is a real danger that actions wholly perfect in the days of His flesh may be a travesty of His character if reproduced slavishly or without regard to changes of environment.

It is of course notorious that a mere quotation of Biblical phrases can result in grotesque parodies of religion: the Devil can quote Scripture, and ill-advised human beings can be almost as perversely ingenious. Though it is of supreme importance to study and interpret the records of Jesus, our purpose in so doing will be to enter into His mind and outlook rather than to find a formula that settles our conduct. During the war and since its close a vast amount of debate has been centred upon certain of His words and deeds: His dealings with centurions, His cleansing of the Temple with "a scourge of small cords," His advice to sell the cloak and buy the sword, His reply "It is enough"—the exact exegesis and permanent significance of these and many other passages have been canvassed by those who hoped to find in them a ruling for or against pacifism. It is untrue to say that such attempts have been irrelevant: they have made it impossible for certain extremists on both sides to claim the authority of His command for their views. But to many of us the whole discussion has always seemed necessarily indecisive, partly because Christian character must be judged by motive rather than by act, but chiefly because the best course in any given position can only be determined by a delicate appreciation of the whole circumstances. The example of Jesus in the Gospels gives us abundant proof of the sensitiveness and variety of His methods. It is easy to collect instances of His gentleness and of His severity so superficially contrasted as to produce an appearance of inconsistency. It is only those who recognize that love's way cannot be cut and dried, that personal relationships cannot be formulated in legal terms, and that what is right in one case may be less than right in another, who can appreciate the depth and wholeness of His character.

Christians throughout the ages have, of course, recognized that the *Imitatio Christi* could not be lightly undertaken, and that the individual believer's "liberty of prophesying" must be checked by the guidance of the fellowship. But even here the interpretation of the Christian's duty in the past is not of itself a final guide. We may agree with Dr. C. J.

SCOPE AND IMPORTANCE OF THE SUBJECT

Cadoux* that in the first three centuries the Church decisively condemned warfare and insisted upon an uncompromising abstention from political or military activities. Or we may agree with St. Thomas Aquinas or with the thirty-seventh Article of Religion that "it is lawful for Christian men, at the commandment of the Magistrate, to wear weapons and serve in the wars." Neither authority is necessarily relevant. For it is at least arguable that conduct appropriate to Christians when the Church was a persecuted minority, or in times when warfare was wholly different from what it is to-day, cannot supply an exact precedent for a radically different situation.

This whole matter must be treated more fully later. Here it may be well to illustrate our main contention, that the best possible course for modern men cannot be settled by determining the best possible course for previous generations. A classic instance, in some ways closely parallel, may be found in the matter of the ministry of women. It would be generally admitted that in the time of our Lord, or indeed at any period until the present, the ordination of women to the Christian ministry would have been not only undesirable but mistaken. So long as woman's status was definitely one of subjection, so long as the Christian conviction that "in Christ is neither male nor female," remained an ideal unattained and save in rare cases unattainable, a grant of equality would have been unjust and impracticable. Now that the whole position of womanhood has been

* *The Early Church and the World.*

altered, a new situation has been created and new possibilities are opened. The very principles which have hitherto postponed equality now demand its achievement. Without denouncing the past we can only be true to its best spirit if we drastically change its policy.

Every change in the human environment thus demands a revision of the content of Christian conduct, a fresh attempt to think out and to apply the principles of Christ. Whether or no war has ever been right for a Christian in the past, the present situation is so manifestly unparalleled that precedent, however universal or august, cannot decide the issue. We have got to work out afresh our interpretation of the Christian's duty, have got to face the possibility that now an obligation previously and perhaps justifiably ignored has become binding, have got to bring whatever we can of spiritual insight and intellectual honesty to the understanding of God's will.

IV

This task of adjusting the appropriate Christian response to the changing environment is obviously as wide as life itself. Indeed, one chief cause of our present weakness is that every aspect of life has been so rapidly and so significantly changed in the past century that Christians have been unable to keep pace with the demands upon them. It is a commonplace that man's opportunities and needs have at present outrun his powers of appreciating and responding to them; that humanity is perplexed by the disparity between its tasks and its resources; that having attained what might be a new world it is unable to bring to its service new vision and new resolve. The complexity and the interdependence, not less than the novelty, of modern problems are sufficient to daunt even the most resolute. We cannot strip ourselves of habits of thought and types of conduct which are in fact anachronisms, nor easily concentrate upon any one issue amid so many.

It is this dilemma that gives its special importance to the problem of war. For here is that which we fail to find elsewhere, a concrete issue that can to some degree be isolated and brought into a manageable compass. In most of the great corporate issues of the time the policy of a limited objective is impracticable. Christians may agree for example that the whole method of speculative finance is morally unsound, that dealings which involve ruthless competition and many of the worst features of gambling, and are almost inseparable from highly coloured advertising, cannot be rendered ethical by an insistence upon the maxim *caveat emptor*. Yet short of a sweeping and simultaneous change in the system, a change that can only be brought about by the co-operation of a vast number of agents, it is difficult if not impossible for the individual to take and keep a standard of conduct worthy of his religion. He may live blamelessly within the code: but where the code is itself sub-Christian he is almost bound either to acquiesce or to abandon his career. If this seems an attack upon an honourable calling, it may be pointed out that we are all in similar case partakers in other men's sins and constrained to work out our allegiance to Christ in circumstances which make almost inevitable a measure of compromise. The man who protests that he has a clear conscience is usually the man who is blind alike to the iniquity of corporate life and to the moral demands of Christ.

Nor can a "step by step" method, by which certain demonstrable evils are selected and the efforts of reformers concentrated upon them, be recommended without reserve. To do so is usually to give the impression that full Christian discipleship can be defined in terms of a few specified obligations; that attention to these can take the place of a radical and complete transformation of nature; and that Christian life consists not in surrender to the Spirit of Christ but in particular acts of religious or ethical obedience. After the C.O.P.E.C. Conference there was a strong temptation to fling the whole weight of the movement into a campaign for the housing of the people. The monstrous evils of slumdom were manifest; the public conscience was already aroused; a concerted effort would have raised no divisive issues and might have rallied the Churches into active and united support. I remember well my own hesitations at that time. Here was an opportunity to right a grievous wrong, a wrong which as a Londoner by birth and training had been always present with me. Here was a concrete task;

in the discharge of it the tense emotion of the Conference might find its release. Almost all my colleagues felt that our long discussions ought to lead to a strong call to action and that this was the most urgent and practicable field. Yet, for a reason that at first I could not define, the proposal left me dissatisfied—instinctively sure that to accept it would be a betrayal. It was not that I thought housing unimportant: I had been working for the previous six months over a housing scheme for my own parish. But C.O.P.E.C. had been demanding radical and revolutionary changes in the whole attitude of Christians, had been insisting on the need for consistent and adventurous thinking, had been striving to see the whole sphere of corporate life in the light of God. To canalize its message into an appeal for slum clearance would be too easy and popular a result. It would allay whatever divine discontent the Conference had aroused, would excuse its members for shirking harder and less congenial issues, would score a cheap success at the cost of renouncing the essential purpose of our work. The searching and difficult issues which we had raised would be conveniently forgotten in a burst of popular approval. It would not do. If C.O.P.E.C. did not result in slum clearance it would have failed: it would have failed still more discreditably if it resulted in slum clearance alone. If a single limited objective was to be chosen, only the cause of peace was large and exacting enough to be a worthy expression of our studies.

In those days the effort to arouse a widespread and united campaign for peace failed—largely, with sorrow be it said, because of the disunion of the Peace Societies and the weakness of the World Alliance. But our attempt to rally them made its contribution to the increase of pacifist activity, and what was then impossible ought now to be less difficult. In any case it is a task that should be repeated.

For it is clear both from history and from psychology that growth depends upon the concurrence of two necessary conditions. There must first be strong vitality, an energy of life expressing itself in the vision of an unattained ideal, in the desire to realize it, and in unrest, discontent, and frustration so long as the desire is unsatisfied. There must also be a particular and worthy opportunity, large enough to satisfy idealism and definite enough to encourage action; an opportunity that is a first step towards the land of dreams, a step difficult enough to demand and evoke power, a step manifestly in the right direction and naturally involving further progress.

Ever since 1918 many of us have been looking for the appearance of this second condition. Despite constant testimony and some evidence to the contrary we do not believe that the general level of idealism is seriously low. It may be that the particular generation which was old enough to feel the horror of war but too young to take part in it has been spoiled. Certainly the rebellions of its more vocal representatives have much of the extravagance of hysteria. It may be that the survivors among its seniors are too few and too overstrained for effective energy. But anyone who knows the solid and uncomplaining courage with which the vast majority of ordinary folk and especially of the professional and working classes have faced the bitter hardships of the past fifteen years will find it difficult to denounce them as degenerate. All over the country are thousands of groups working together in the effort to clarify and express their yearning for newness of life, studying, discussing, serving, organizing, praying for human welfare. Some of them may be cranky and perverse; some wrong-headed and misled; all in some degree perplexed and unsatisfied. But they contain among them a mass of fine religious aspiration, and a power of sacrifice which only waits for a clear objective.

To unify and release this potential reserve of energy is perhaps the supreme business of the Church. General appeals are too vague to arouse enthusiasm—though if they can be simplified as they have been by the Oxford Group their power is manifest. Concrete duties—education, the service of the unemployed, sex ethics, international friendship, foreign missions—although all of them demand attention and present new problems and opportunities, appeal only to a limited number, and important as they are cannot strike the required note of urgency. The cause of peace, obviously essential to the saving of civilization, obviously incumbent upon every follower of Christ, obviously and for the first time practicable, might serve as the attractive impulse which should give coherence and expression to the latent and spasmodic desires of mankind. For the Church its response to that cause may well be the test of its survival—*articulus stantis aut cadentis ecclesiae*.

V

One further preliminary must be discussed. If the importance of the pacifist problem is so evident and typical, and if ever since August 1914 it has been hotly debated, are we not driven to one of two conclusions—either that the solution of it is obvious although men may refuse to accept it, or that the issue is insoluble and that no measure of agreement upon it can be expected? In any case is it worth while prolonging the debate?

In a sense any question of such magnitude and so intimately connected with the whole difficulty of life can never be finally answered. Certainly the present writer has no confidence in his power to solve it. But there are obvious reasons which explain why despite so much debate progress has been slow, and why there is now perhaps a fairer chance of success.

All of us who took part in the "peace or war" arguments during and immediately after the war will agree that the atmosphere made dispassionate enquiry and unexaggerated statement almost impossible. Feelings ran too strong: the wounds whether of prison or of the trenches were still raw: pacifists could not forget the way in which they had been reviled, brow-beaten, persecuted: ex-service men could not forgive the fact that they had faced death while others for whatever reasons had made no such sacrifice. In consequence argument was always charged with emotions of the strongest kinds. It took nearly as long for the conscientious objector to realize that all soldiers were not pagans as it did for the soldier to learn that all "conchies" were not cowards. Even when generosity and friendship and the pursuit of a common end made speech easy, it was hard to avoid opening up old scars or reviving memories of exquisite agony. The pacifist could not state his case without condemning or seeming to condemn those who had shared in war: the soldier could hardly explain his position without seeming to glorify a bloody business which he had no wish to defend.

To some extent that difficulty still remains. It is probably the common experience—I have felt it continually—that very few statements, whether pacifist or not, give us any sort of satisfaction. If I may be frank, when I listen to some of my peace-loving friends, their arguments arouse an instinctive antagonism: their horror of death, the falsity of their picture of war, their failure to recognize the existence of human beings whose religion glorifies fighting, their inability to resist the appeal to fear and to disgust, as if Satan could ever cast out Satan —these things merely fill me with a vast admiration for the simple heroism of the lads whom I buried somewhere in France. To read even so sincere and passionate a *cri du coeur* as Mr. Beverley Nichols's *Cry Havoc* is to be constantly reminded of the neurosis from which he is manifestly suffering. Sensitive, imaginative, courageous as he is, one cannot forget that poignant scene in Savernake when he parted from his schoolfellow so soon to be slain, or the confession of a much greater sufferer, "It is only those who have not themselves suffered who have a morbid horror of pain." Believing as I do that his cause is right, eager as I am to see the world set ablaze for peace, there are far too many passages in his book which provoke in me a deep intuitive impulse to say with Mr. Yeats Brown, "the mass of mankind, thank God, is not pacifist."

Yet in the other camp my fate is even more certain. Set me to listen to the apologists for war—I do not mean to the swashbucklers of the *Daily Express*, but to distinguished Christian statesmen—and all my soul cries out in protest. If this cautious and lukewarm conventionality is the best that the Church can do, if we are to haggle about the perils of unilateral disarmament while all the world is waiting for a lead, if despite all our phrases the appeal is in the last resort to the sword, then such advocates are welcome to try the trenches: I shall not be there. Do these people really suppose that the fighting soldier enjoyed battle? Do they forget that the one clear aim for which men died and women agonized was a world safe for democracy, a world where war should be no more? If not, how can they be so compromising in their praise of peace, so afraid of being labelled pacifist, so acquiescent in the lie that readiness for war is an insurance against it? Better the nightmares of Mr. Nichols, better any sort of crazy pacifism, than "the wisdom of this world, earthly, sensual, devilish," than the caution which prides itself upon seeing both sides of a question and thinks that the function of a leader is to chair committees and see that they reach inoffensive results. "Go slow" may be a wise man's motto: it is exactly what the Pharisees must have said when Jesus appeared before the Sanhedrin.

The plain fact is (I am afraid) that for my generation the only folks who can discuss war are the people who saw it at close quarters, and most of them prefer to keep quiet. Even when they do, there is of course no very strong agreement. Of the books and plays *Journey's End* is far more like my own experience than any other that I have read: every incident and character in it could have been paralleled from my own battalions. Yet many who had seen service in other months or places regarded it as completely unreal. Probably they are right and I am wrong: for hitherto the only man whose judgment of war exactly agreed with my own was a German ex-gunner, who had helped to shell me out of the Cambrai salient in November 1917.

It may, of course, be urged that an exact understanding of war and of its effect upon those who took part in it is really unnecessary. We are agreed that it is evil: we are agreed that the glamour and romance attached to it in the past are now wholly false: our concern should be to replace fascination by loathing. Barbusse, Remarque, and the realists who are not afraid to be brutal and can create an atmosphere of horror—these are enough. Those who point to other sides of the picture will only seem to palliate and in so doing perpetuate the iniquity. Exaggeration is excusable in propaganda.

That is, of course, sufficient reason for the plea that if we are to get rid of war we must try to form a truthful verdict upon it. Granted that there is urgent need for what Mr. Mencken calls "de-bunking," too violent assault here as in literary criticism is apt to overreach itself. The onslaught upon "Eminent Victorians" is already producing a reaction: a similar fate may well overtake the work of those for whom war is merely nauseous. A negative attitude based on dread and disgust will not have power to cast out war: only an understanding of it and the provision of an alternative which surpasses whatever worth there is in it, will succeed in overthrowing it.

Yet even so the difficulty of a just valuation remains. Mr. Nichols sets side by side the famous sonnet by Rupert Brooke and a lurid snapshot by Mr. Siegfried Sassoon, and asks which we should choose to impress upon our children. The answer is a question for experts in educational psychology, and is not, to my mind, so obvious as it is to Mr. Nichols. But if we ask which picture is the more true, we must not forget that though neither is a complete verdict each represents the salient mood of the time at which it was written. It was exactly with Brooke's wistful gallantry that the "first hundred thousand" set out upon their adventure. Until Loos that spirit survived. It did not give way to the dogged martyrdom of the later years until after the blood-bath of the Somme. That hideous holocaust and the still more horrible futility of Passchendaele in the following year stripped the last rags of glamour from battle. No wonder the boys who after two or three years of tremulous expectation were flung for the first time into such horror carried away nothing but loathing. At school they had been fed on the valour of the embusqués and the well-meant cheerfulness of those whose business it was to kindle their ardour: but they had seen the casualty lists and on them name after name of their seniors: they could not face their ordeal in the blissful ignorance of the lads of 1914. At the beginning war seemed like a game, at the end it was manifestly a shambles. That must not be forgotten when we estimate its literature.

The importance and difficulty of this valuation of warfare may perhaps excuse an element of autobiography in this book; indeed, my own experience during and since the war is the chief reason for its appearance. To have seen active service in various phases of the struggle and to have come to a thorough-going pacifism as a result of it is not indeed uncommon: but it should enable a certain detachment and balance of judgment not usually prominent in discussions. My intention is to examine the religious and ethical problem, not to produce propaganda. Probably the result will disappoint and irritate. Certain issues which seem obvious to many are to me difficult and obscure: certain methods of advocacy on both sides, powerful as may be their emotional appeal, seem to me unworthy and deplorable: certain aspersions both upon the soldier and the conscientious objector I know to be false: certain pictures of peace look almost more unattractive than war; certain pictures of war are nightmare and neurasthenia. If there is any strength in my plea for peace—for the outlawry of war, for disarmament, for the refusal to fight—it will arise from the fact that I have seen war without horror and can appreciate and share its appeal to mankind.

In these days when the popular Press treats the scientist as a sort of medicine-man and exploits public ignorance and fear in the interest of the armament firms, it is doubly important for the advocates of peace to avoid exaggeration. Lurid pictures of London as a reeking shambles and of Britain drenched in unknown poisons by a single flight of aeroplanes may be permissible to Mr. Edgar Wallace: the shilling shocker has a legitimate place among the lower grades of literature, though the masters of the art have long ago banned death rays and Borgia rings and secret chemicals. Warfare is ghastly enough without being decked in the panoply of the witch-doctor: we shall do disservice to the future if we let either its glamour or its gruesomeness distort our outlook. So let the following memories be set in comparison with the chapter of *Cry Havoc* in which Mr. Beverley Nichols describes his visit to the Gas-mask Factory, and his feelings on entering the gas-chamber*—one of the most poignant and fear-inspiring passages in recent literature. I wish I had his power of language or of emotion.

On July 12, 1917, the battalion of Royal Fusiliers to which I was attached was on the Cambrin sector south of the La Bassée canal. It was a "peace front"; for we had been cut up at Oppy Wood two months before and were far below strength. I was living with A Company in a tunnel dug-out in Old Boots Trench. At midnight the senior subaltern came in from his round of the posts, reported "All quiet," and suggested that we turn in. For the last time, as events proved, I stripped and got into pyjamas, and was wriggling into my sleeping-bag when a dull flat explosion interrupted me. It was almost on the mouth of our dug-out, and was the first splash of a deluge. Gas, obviously; and an immediate smarting of the eyes. We had heard rumours of phosgene, as new and scentless, and usually mixed with lachrymatory. It was now pouring down the stairs onto our bunks.

No time to change. Slip on a mask, fit the nose-clip, chew the tube, tie the strings. Let down the blanket over the entrance. Get into a pair of shoes. Wait for the next job.

* For the relatively ineffective effects of gas in war, cf. a lecture by Dr. F. A. Freeth, F.R.S., reported in *The Times*, January 27, 1934.

Tinkle of a trench telephone. My companion must unmask and answer in an atmosphere reeking with poison. Battalion Headquarters talking—anxious for news—is it the prelude to a raid? Hard to report when the two of us and an orderly are alone and right under the shelling.

Subaltern must stay at his post: my job is to get to B.H.Q. and act as messenger. Up the steps, past the curtain, into the wreckage of the trench—in pyjamas and pumps, a gas-mask, and a tin hat—almost suffocated and quite unable to see. Try half an hour in a mask if you doubt it. One's face perspires; the sweat gets into the tube and fogs the eye-pieces.

Fortunately I knew the trench night or day; had practised walking the zig-zag; had counted the traverses to the alley that led to H.Q. Crash! A bit of corrugated iron had fallen across it; hit me on the bridge of the nose; cut a shallow gash. Much blood but nothing to matter.

Obviously the mask must come off, if I am ever to arrive. Bad enough to keep on stubbing one's toes; no use cutting one's head open. So at speed through the gas along the duck-boards.

H.Q. at last. Colonel's face a study—a pink and blood-stained ghost, helmeted and mask adangle, fronting him at the salute. "Good God, it's the padre," and a shout of relieved laughter. "Come to report, sir. Officers gone to the posts: men standing-to. Shelling seems purely local, probably at the heavy Toc Emma behind Bay 74 Old Boots." A few sentences of instruction; a drink; and back to the Company.

In Old Boots a lad sick and choking, unable to move, one stretcher-bearer trying to carry him. "Get a stretcher: I'll take an end. Down Maison Rouge to the aid-post." An hour or two carrying casualties from the front line. Not very many, but a ghastly business. Then to the dug-out.

"Phosgene, how does it work?" "Is it head or heart or lungs or skin that goes?" "Effect not immediate—gets you an hour or two later—no preliminary symptoms—just snuffs you out." So we argued, the four of us reassembled there. "We've all been drenched with it: we're all done in." "Steady: we're not dead yet." When you have spent a night with a bunch of lads who knew that they had been poisoned, Mr. Nichols's shudders seem a trifle cheap.

Next day I fainted once or twice, saw the doctor, was warned to go sick or go slow; and have never been able to play cricket with comfort since. But others died.

That is a gas attack.

Or this:

November 30, 1917, with the 1st Berkshires in the Cambrai salient, outside the sugar factory at Graincourt cross-road, when that day's battle was nearly done—a grim and critical day, whereof see the C.-in-C.'s dispatch. I was trying to collect the wounded and say a prayer over the dead.

A burst of shells, a sneeze, gas and probably

deadly, for they don't send over sneezing-mixture for fun. A rush to get the mask on, to fit the clip on the nostrils—sneeze and a gasp for breath; try again—sneeze and another lungsful of whatever poison is about. Some twenty times that performance repeated itself: as soon as the clip touched my nose it was blown away by an uncontrollable explosion. I was too scared to sneeze and then seize the mouthpiece for the intake; indeed, so violent was the paroxysm that I doubt if it would have been possible. Twenty times and each time a race with death: comic to look back upon, but some of us, however dull our imaginations, know what it is to be afraid.

And my colleagues wonder why I don't care for snuff.

CHAPTER II

THE CONFLICT OF LOYALTIES

I

IF the issue, peace or war, is testing, it is also typical —representative of a multitude of problems in which a conflict of loyalties lies at the heart of the difficulty. Christian discipleship is not easy even for the saints; for us ordinary sinners it is enormously hard: indeed, when a man begins to talk glibly of absolute honesty or absolute love it is fairly evident that he is very young and has neither thought deeply nor prayed earnestly. Is it Christian for me to spend more than the average income, to draw money from investments or tithe, to enjoy my dinner at a College high table, to buy new delphiniums or new dress clothes, to send my son to a public school, to accept preferment in the Church, to repeat the Athanasian Creed? There may be an affirmative answer to such questions: but to ignore them or to think that the answer is simple is only possible if one's conscience is dull or one's intelligence defective. And beyond them lie others in which the art of living Christianly in a world like this has to be discovered.

There before me stands the Bishop of Gloucester's question, "How would Christ have acted?" At my best, in rare moments of self-forgetfulness and inspiration, I have had a glimpse of what St. Paul's gospel of life "in Christ" might mean. But to fulfil those glimpses demands a power of love, a clearness of mind, a strength of will that is altogether beyond me. There must be passion, the passion of a great devotion that casts out fear and every selfish ambition and fixes purpose in an inevitable constraint. But there must also be mental effort; for the issues that call for action are complex, and to suppose that we can solve them by instinct or passive obedience is to gainsay our human status. The obligation to Christ has to be fulfilled in the discharge of other and often conflicting obligations; for man is never an isolated individual, and every contact with his fellows and environment sets up its own claim upon him. As son or parent, worker or employer, consumer, citizen, Churchman, each one of us accepts responsibilities which involve opportunities for compromise and for apostasy.

The wider aspects of the conflict of loyalties will engage our attention later. For concrete illustration and study of it the problem of pacifism is an excellent and typical case. Twenty years of intense debate should have provided material for its discussion: its subject is of universal and immediate importance: courses of conduct depend upon its decision: the Christian has a special duty to consider it. Moreover, though it goes deep, it is relatively simple: factors which in less familiar or less definite fields are hard to analyse can here be disentangled. In consequence, if we can isolate the issue a decision here should help to similar decisions in cognate

THE CONFLICT OF LOYALTIES 51

subjects, and so to clearer understanding of the Christian ethic in the modern world.

It has, of course, long been recognized that discussion of the pacifist claims raised arguments of general significance: indeed, many of us have at times protested against treating the issue as isolated and independent. We felt that the principles asserted by many advocates of peace would logically involve a complete withdrawal from all corporate life, a Tolstoyan renunciation of all contact with organized society. To denounce compromise at this point and to admit it elsewhere seemed to us merely inconsistent. If war was evil, so was competitive capitalism. When a great chocolate manufacturer asserted that all war was unchristian, but that industry was public service for human welfare, we could not but invite him to act up to his faith and publish for the benefit of mankind the secret processes on which the wealth of his firm depended. His refusal to do so, however natural, seemed to cast a slur upon the sincerity of his pacifism. To indict conflict in one sphere, and to indulge in it in another, required explanation—especially for those of us who found the qualities of militarists less unchristian than those of millionaires, and the ethics of propaganda identical with those of advertisement.

But if the step by step method is defensible, such objections are not hard to meet. No one supposes that war is the only evil in life: many would hesitate to say that it is the worst of evils. The cause of peace is only one stage in the Christian adventure:

there are other and not less difficult tasks ahead. But peace happens to be the issue on which at present others depend: we cannot deal with them until the dread of war has been removed. Moreover, as we shall try to show hereafter, a point has now been reached in which we can legitimately treat war as an anachronism. Those of us who are most conscious that the evils of competitive capitalism are as manifest and not less unclean, may yet agree that it is in the campaign against war that we must first engage against them.

A parallel from the last great Christian adventure may reassure us. To many of his contemporaries, as for example to Cobbett, it seemed perverse that William Wilberforce should concentrate his energies upon negro slavery. To them it seemed less immediate and less iniquitous than the enslavement of women and children in British mines and mills. Yet in liberating the slaves Wilberforce appealed to certain principles which once admitted could not be restricted in their application. If human freedom was a sacred right, if persons must not be treated as chattels, then a revaluation of life was begun; and the energies evoked for the negro must be applied to similar efforts for his fellow-labourers at home. It is not an accident that the victory of the liberator was the prelude to the work of Shaftesbury and Maurice, to factory acts and public education, to franchise reform and the co-operative movement. The conscience of mankind had been aroused to a fuller understanding of brotherhood: an advance

THE CONFLICT OF LOYALTIES

in one part of the field led on to progress elsewhere.

Such an illustration reveals a universal rule of conduct. "Take hold of it at the nearest point," said Loch to an enquirer who asked him how to begin a life of social service: "The issues are so vast that it doesn't matter where you start: until you've made the plunge it all seems hopelessly bewildering: once you've started, you'll never be able to stop." War for us at our particular moment seems the proper point of approach.

II

Once upon a time, in the early days after the war, the Archbishops' Recruiting Campaign sent me to tour the Rural Deaneries of Suffolk. It was an attempt, the first of many, to enlist the enthusiasm that the years of struggle had revealed for the service of the world-wide missionary adventure. Its object was to supply a moral equivalent: its slogan was "Christ or Chaos."

In those days our method was simple. We painted a picture of the new age with all its possibilities of peril: we reminded our hearers of their dreams and pledges, of the horrors that had been temporarily ended but might so easily return: we challenged them to find a way of salvation: we pointed confidently but somewhat vaguely to Christ. It was all transparently sincere: we believed what we said, even if our rhetoric was more impressive than our logic. Before I had time to wonder why the appeal was not more successful, a chance utterance from the back of a hall put an end to easy speech.

He was a small, elderly man; and he asked a question. "I agree with everything that our speaker has said. I've longed all my life, and tried all I can, to live as a Christian. Will he tell me what to do? I'm in business—got a grocer's shop down the street. If I ran it on the lines of the Kingdom of God, if I gave up the tricks of the trade, if I told the naked truth, I'd be broke in six months. I've got a wife and girls dependent on me. What am I to do?"

Simple enough to preach the duty of following Christ: less simple to tell a man to follow in scorn of consequence: desperately hard to send him and his family to martyrdom, when he was so honest and so frank. Was I as honest and as frank? If so, should not I be alongside him, facing the same prospect? What are you to do when your ideal of conduct calls you one way, and your love of others, your duty to your circle, calls you another, when you want to follow Christ and don't want to be a prig or involve others against their will in pain? Let him that is without sin among us cast the first stone.

That was the event that set me working at C.O.P.E.C.: there the trivial case that revealed the futility of a merely individualistic Christianity. For obviously, unless a man was prepared to cut himself off from social contacts, he must be a partaker in other men's sins until society was wholly Christian. Most of us escape such a conflict of loyalties by cultivating moral insensitiveness. We buy goods without enquiring into the conditions of their manufacture. We draw dividends without responsibility for the way in which they are obtained. We consume more than our share of the world's wealth without any sense of shame or of obligation. If we are challenged, our reply is that of the first murderer, "Am I my brother's keeper?" When we become sensitive, we have to face the conflict. Is it possible to follow Christ all the way, or is there a proper place for compromise? The gravity of that question must be realized.

It will not be forgotten that it was raised with reference to Christ Himself in one of the most poignant of recent books about Him.* Dr. Klausner, a learned and sympathetic Jewish Rabbi, after striving to show how much the teaching of Jesus had in common with contemporary Judaism, faces the question why He was rejected and condemned. He finds the reason for it in the unpractical and anarchic idealism of Jesus, and argues that His ethics if followed would destroy the foundations of social, industrial, and political life. Family ties, commercial acumen, patriotic citizenship are the basis of man's ordered progress: ignore or override them, and civilization falls into chaos. Yet Jesus explicitly challenges them. Such idealism may be theoretically magnificent: if accepted it would be immediately disastrous. Which is the better and more honourable course—to face the issue as the

* *Jesus of Nazareth* (George Allen & Unwin Ltd.).

Jews faced it and refuse to follow an illusion; or to profess discipleship and then as Christians have done quietly forsake all that it involves? Judaism may have acted brutally when it condemned the Nazarene: at least it was honest. Can this be said of the Church? Was it not contemptible to profess allegiance, to evade all its difficult demands, and to adopt an attitude of complacent superiority on the strength of cowardice and compromise? Lip-service and protestations of devotion consort ill with worldly wisdom and practical apostasy. Few of his readers could have felt that such a judgment was wholly unjust.

This is in fact the charge, seldom expressed but very widely felt, which honest enquirers bring against the Church to-day. They see a great gulf fixed between Christian profession and Christian practice; and the contrast suggests at best hypocrisy and at worst a depraving of all moral and intellectual worth. In a generation taught by science to value sincerity it seems intolerable to proclaim a Cross and grasp at a Crown, to build shrines in honour of the poor man of Nazareth and to enjoy comfort, strive for money, wage war in His name.

An intelligent Hindu comes to London, attracted by what he has seen of Christian missionaries in India, assured by them of the advantages of Christian civilization, and expecting to find a Christian city. We know too well how bitter is his disillusionment. He looks for love, joy, peace as the fruit of the Spirit: he finds blatant egoism, ruthless competition, luxury and profligacy at one end, squalor and misery at the other. He goes to the Abbey and hears of Jesus Christ: he comes out and concludes that Christianity is one vast imposture, that Christians are either fools or knaves, that the Church is expert only in making the best of both worlds. He may perhaps find evidence that there is a remnant not wholly insincere: but how small and weak against the dominance of Mammon.

A similar verdict is expressed with more or less reluctance by a majority of our fellow-countrymen; and at times everyone of us must have felt compelled to assent to it. There is a moment in the lives of all thinking Christians when the contrast strikes home upon them and leaves them numbed and shattered. They have felt the beauty of Christ: they have caught the infection of His claims: they want to surrender their lives to Him: they believe in the mission of His Church and the integrity of its ministers. Then some small fact reveals what appears the hollow fraudulence of it. These church-workers so assiduous in their devotions, so venomous in their jealousies and gossip. These seat-holders, so proud of their support of the Church, and of their incomes and social status, their good works and their worldly success. These clergy who walk in vestments and love salutations in the market-place and the chief seats at feasts—and don't they get annoyed if due respect is not paid to their cloth! "Scribes and Pharisees, hypocrites," how can he escape that conclusion or fail to see the deadly parallels in the

Gospels? In youth, when our eyes are still clear, we notice these things and are shocked; and the conflict of loyalties becomes acute.

It is the same conflict that underlies the whole bitter irony. Few men are wilfully insincere: most of us could honestly repudiate a charge of hypocrisy. But with us as with the Pharisees convention has blinded our vision: we have persuaded ourselves that we can best serve by accepting the code of "good form," that progress is slow and must not be revolutionary, that we can leaven society by adopting its traditions; and before we realize it our moral perception has lost its edge, vested interests have set fetters upon our freedom, popularity has become synonymous with love, and the herd instinct either dominates us or drives us into an aggressive self-assertion. In any case the impulse to follow Christ is rationalized into a system which seems both to satisfy our religious obligations and to leave us free for acquisitiveness and egoism.

At times, and the outbreak of war was one of them, a great issue forces us to a decision. We have made terms with the world on the ordinary matters of conduct. Here is something extraordinary, to which the rules of caution and compromise have not been habitually applied. Hitherto we have managed to combine loyalty to Christ with loyalty to Caesar—generally by obscuring the contrast between them. Now the question "Who is on the Lord's side? Who?" is forced upon our attention. We must make a decision, or at least consider what being on the Lord's side means. We will discuss the problem in its personal reference later. Here it is sufficient to say that just as our Hindu finds it impossible to reconcile Christian faith with the practices of Christians, so the mass of mankind during and since the war has been convinced that the Church cannot reconcile its official conduct in those years with its professed imitation of Christ. They feel that the Church claims to guide the life of mankind and that some sections of it at least insist upon the possession of an authority supernatural and inerrant; that here was a crisis in which the Church far from guiding public opinion capitulated to national passions and used its influence to condone or even to justify evil; that its credit is bankrupt in consequence.

III

At the outbreak of war those of us who were of military age were faced with an inevitable decision, and in most cases a very typical instance of the conflict of loyalties. To go or to stay may seem an easy choice to those who look back upon it twenty years later, and in the light of full discussion. In fact it was probably easier than it would be to-day; for most of us simply felt that being what we were we had no option but to go. It will be well to put the case plainly as most of us saw it—confessing that I at least should now give a radically different verdict.

In the first place most of us had never seriously questioned the necessity of war. We had been brought up on school books that glorified it, a view of the Bible which accepted it, and a scientific outlook in which progress and struggle were inseparably linked. Kipling had thrilled our youth; Mafeking had made war look like a game; volunteering had been a dull but unquestioned part of school and college routine. It was not that we were necessarily Tories or Imperialists; painting the map red already seemed rather contemptible. Indeed, many of us were deeply concerned in social service; clubs and settlements were more vigorous than they are to-day; holiday camps, missions, and the Student Movement had a large place in our vacations.

For if we had not questioned war, we simply did not believe that it was possible except on the fringes of civilization. Lord Roberts might deliver warnings; the *Panther* might go to Agadir; in the Balkans strife might be endemic. But in Europe and the great nations it was inconceivable that common sense would not find a way of peace. All this parade of guns and Dreadnoughts, of Life Guards in breastplates and Grenadiers in bearskins, seemed proper to the pageantry of royalty, but remote from a sober and peace-loving age. I remember reading Erskine Childers's fascinating tale *The Riddle of the Sands*, and for all its vivid accuracy it was as unreal as *Rupert of Hentzau*: indeed, when I re-read it in the early weeks of war I could not bring myself to believe that this fantasy, this thriller, this detective story, dealt with dangers that were now actually involving us. In the autumn of 1914 the imagination could hardly picture a war in Western Europe: not till winter and the trenches did we learn to accept it as cold fact, and even then could not believe that it would last beyond the spring.

If it had come unchallenged and unexpected, its glamour was increased by the cause for which we were called to fight. To reopen the question of war guilt is futile: no doubt in a sense our refusal to recognize the possibility was guilt enough; and our motives may have been in fact less pure than we believed. But it is hard to find any war in which it would have been more difficult to abstain, any circumstances in which the case for intervention could be so powerfully pleaded. Our Government was notoriously pacific: its spokesmen, and particularly the Foreign Minister, were neither demagogues nor firebrands. We could be sure that they had not chosen strife in a moment of passion or in response to mass emotion. When they accepted it as inevitable their decision was hard to impugn.

A necessary evil, a catastrophe that we had never foreseen or set ourselves to forestall, a cause for which, if ever, honour and duty and justice called us to fight—was it likely that young men faced with such an appeal would resist it? We had taken advantage of our citizenship in an Empire built up by war: could we repudiate the obligation of citizenship now when the price of Empire had to be paid? We had taken no steps to work against war: could we become pacifists now without inconsistency and cowardice? We were called not to hatred but to sacrifice: could we in so fair a cause preserve our own lives while our comrades were going to their death? Such arguments may seem superficial and inadequate in retrospect. At the time they left us with only one answer to give.

All these arguments had weight. It was the last, in my own case as, I believe, in most others, that drove me to apply for a combatant commission early in August. The impulse to share with our friends the testing of their manhood, although later on it was played upon by propaganda and debased by mass hatred, sprang at first simply from the ties of affection. Men whom we admired and loved were enlisting: they could not be allowed to go alone. Fear of their scorn may have counted for something; emulation of their courage had its place: but mainly it was the feeling that in the ordeal comrades must stand together, that death with them was better than life alone. Those who had known the stronger types of group life found it most difficult to break fellowship in 1914. Loyalty to friends, themselves offering up their lives, prevailed over all other loyalties.

If this was the normal attitude, it is obvious that the normal is sub-Christian. To accept war as inevitable—how is that consistent with clear vision or any sort of Christian faith? To have been insensitive to the risk of war and therefore indifferent to the need of striving to prevent it—that is to have been content with a fool's paradise. To follow human companions without reference to Christ or regard for men of other nations, and to follow them not only to death but to organized killing—is that so very high a loyalty?

There were others, even in 1914, who resisted the pull of all such impulses and chose a different course. They believed—and in many cases had their Quaker heritage to support them—that war was for them an impossible crime and for the nations an insensate folly. They had long regarded it as one of those evils against which the need to protest was urgent. However good the cause—and most of them accepted the cleanness of the country's motives—war seemed to them the wrong method to employ. Duty to friends and country and God would not be served by a display of physical courage, but by fortitude in challenging popular emotion, objecting to any form of military service, and showing the highest loyalty to their fellows by faithfulness to the Christ. They had consistently accepted their status as citizens subject to the right to protest against the government. Indeed, many of them as Free Churchmen were habituated to resisting State demands, and to contrasting their secular with their sacred allegiance. The issue for them could easily be seen as Christ or Caesar, and the history of their churches encouraged them to resist Caesar for his own sake as well as for Christ's. Of such people the majority stood out against enlistment in face of public disapproval, and with the coming of conscription were exposed to the odium, persecution, and imprisonment that was meted out by the Tribunals to the Conscientious Objector. Under long-continued strain it was hard for them to keep free from bitterness and from self-pity.

It would not in fact be true to suggest that on the outbreak of war Christian opinion found itself sharply divided, with the Established Church supporting the State and the Free Churches criticizing it. There were Anglicans who took and maintained a pacifist position: apart from the Society of Friends there was no denomination solidly or even largely pacifist—Congregationalism being probably the most inclined to protest. But it was evident that a man's general religious outlook had a powerful influence. Those in whom the sense of independence, of individual responsibility, and of a prophetic ministry was strong, naturally refused to accept civic obligation without scrutiny. Those whose religion involved the discipline of membership in a corporate fellowship, who were accustomed to obeying an ordered liturgy and clerical leadership, and who could not regard Church and State as antagonistic powers, found it equally natural to respond to that obligation with alacrity. In the new alignment of Christians created by the impact of the new knowledge it is often difficult not to feel that the distinction between Anglican and Nonconformist has lost its meaning: even the matter of Establishment is no longer acutely debated. But the discussions in the early months of the war showed that there was a deep-seated divergence in the emphasis placed respectively upon corporate solidarity and individual responsibility. Anglicans, even if not ready to assert the divine authority of "the powers that be," saw it as their duty to preserve unity even at the cost of sacrificing private judgment. Free Churchmen, if not avowedly prejudiced against accepting secular decisions, were on their guard against any submission which should infringe the liberty of the individual conscience. As the history both of Christendom and of Christians shows, the adjustment of the claims of these conflicting interests is a matter of the most acute difficulty. A freedom which shall escape moral anarchy, an obedience which stops short of acquiescence in evil, represent an ideal hard to define or to sustain.

IV

Before we examine more closely the analysis of the conflict, attention must be directed to those who found a middle way practicable. For this attitude was not only strongly represented by many non-Christians, but was typical of certain influential spokesmen of the Churches, and still survives widespread.

Was the issue really so clean cut? Was there no choice except prison or the trenches? Was it not possible while approving the national action and supporting the nation's cause to confine support to methods which would not involve a direct share in the beastliness of organized murder?

It is not easy, for one who saw only a plain alternative, to sympathize with those who thus appeared able to make the best of both worlds. Of the young men who sought work of national importance or the security and decorations of a Government office, he can hardly write without prejudice. But he has no desire to intrude upon ground which Mr. C. E. Montague made his own: the heroes of *Honours Easy* have had justice done to them by his *saeva indignatio*; and some of them hardly deserve it. There can be little satisfaction in watching from a safe distance the agony of a crucified world. It is because this attitude had a fatal attraction for many Christians and may well be repeated in future that it must be considered.

For some time I collected and kept a number of replies given by prominent Churchmen to young clergy and ministers who sought counsel from them. A few were outspoken: "You stand for Christ in a world that needs to hear His voice: your task will be hard—to maintain a Christian outlook when passion runs high, to keep free from bitterness and hate, to maintain your own vision while not denouncing others"; or "if you are honestly convinced that your Cross is that of military service, and if you can leave your work at home without serious damage to it, the cause is one for which a man should be prepared to die: go with my blessing." The most part tried, at great length and with much equivocal phrasing, to evade the dilemma. In effect what they usually said could be reduced to this: "it is a holy cause—never forget to insist upon that, and to help your people to respond to it: but for a Christian minister there is a holier service than fighting: you are needed to comfort the mourners, to sustain the morale of the civil population, to evoke the resources of prayer, to encourage a spirit of sacrifice"—or in cruder terms "this is a holy war: your hands are too holy for bloodshed: you may serve in the ambulance or recruiting departments—a useful, necessary but not dangerous occupation." That was an answer very frequently given: it is one which I have always found difficult to defend or even to understand—perhaps because I saw and shared the distress that it caused.

Yet here as with all positions sincerely held, a defence is possible. Granted that war is inevitable at our present stage of development and that a particular war is in defence of a just cause, active resistance to it, if not wrong, has merely the effect of prolonging its agony and weakening the side whose victory would be for the best. Christians must deplore the struggle, must assert that it would be impossible in a Christian world, must point out that it is in definite ways a failure in discipleship. But as the lesser of two evils they can support it and encourage enlistment in it. That a class in the community should devote itself to upholding a high ideal even when its immediate attainment is impracticable, and to keeping the nation's soul from bitterness and flagrant apostasy, will be to the benefit both of Church and State. All men are sinners, and to suspend the ministry of the Gospel because their sin involves warfare would be absurd. We cannot fulfil the Sermon on the Mount literally; nor expect men and nations to behave as if earth were heaven. We cannot avoid a measure of compromise; "we must not think ourselves pure above the world."*

It is of course easy to castigate such a position. An "all or nothing" position has the advantage of logical defence. But does not whole-hearted discipleship involve a Tolstoyan abstention from any human activity, or a hermit's refuge from contamination with the world? The arguments that would commit us to absolute pacifism could be used to dispute our right to any place as producers or consumers in modern industrialism, could compel us to renounce one after another all social relationships. Unless we contract out of the system of organized life, it may be difficult to show cause why war should be more offensive to the conscience than any other corporate evil. To discriminate against it may merely involve us in a charge of inconsistency or dishonesty. To keep in touch with one's fellows and with public opinion, striving rather to lift it by sympathy and co-operation than to challenge and denounce it, may not be heroic, but is at least practicable. Did not Christ Himself give us the parable of the leaven, and Himself abstain from passing a verdict upon war or slavery or specific

* Drinkwater, *Abraham Lincoln*, p. 40.

social evils? Indeed, He accepted the society of His time unlike John the Baptist who denounced it and the Essenes who withdrew from it. He sowed a seed which has grown and will grow if we are faithful and patient.

Here then is something like a middle road—the road followed by the majority of Church leaders, at least at the first. If later the recruiting officer tended to prevail over the consoler, none of us who felt the increasing power of mass emotion will be surprised or contemptuous. To defend the weak, to accept responsibility and undergo hardship, to ride loose to life and be ready to lay it down for others, to hold fast the faith that God can "bring good out of evil and make even the wrath of man to turn to His praise"—these are convictions not lightly to be scorned. If we have come to see that there are better ways of defence than military action; that there are higher responsibilities than national obligation and more austere hardships than warfare; that opportunities for romance and sacrifice are not limited to physical conflict; and that to do or acquiesce in evil that good may come brings a just condemnation and a sterile result; yet those who in 1914 had not yet learnt such lessons are only to be blamed if they have remained unteachable.

What seems to be required of us now is that we should reconsider the whole question, using our previous decision as a starting-point but recognizing that the position is now widely different, and that even if we are satisfied that we acted for the best in 1914 we must not for the sake of a desire for consistency or in order to avoid the trouble of further thought let the past be a precedent. War was not so obviously obsolete—was indeed a present reality twenty years ago. These years have revealed its futility, have led politicians not less than Christians to denounce it, and have given us every reason to insist that it is now a manifest anachronism.

It is because so many of us do not seem prepared to make the effort to change our outlook and are drifting into the same state of confusion and apathy which characterized our attitude in 1914 that it is worth while to remind ourselves of those days. Unless we can reach a clearer and truer sense of the issues at stake, we shall see displayed the same uncertainty, the same suggestibility, the same surrender to mob madness, when next a *casus belli* occurs. To recount these old reactions to war should be at once a warning and an incentive.

CHAPTER III

THE PROBLEM OF GUIDANCE

I

It is of course manifest that these decisions of twenty years ago are not now directly relevant. Indeed, the chief contention of this book is that circumstances to-day are in this regard wholly changed, and that the events of the post-war years offer us the possibility of a fresh and quite different decision. But it is important to examine the conflict of loyalties set up in 1914 both because there appear to be many whose outlook is still what it was then, and because the wider problem, how to live Christianly in an unchristian world, concerns us all in daily life and is not solved even in the matter of war because new factors have there arisen.

We turn, therefore, with the data of 1914 in our minds, to examine the question how can the Christian faced with such a decision resolve the tension and bring his creed and his conduct into consistency. To do so is in effect to discuss the question of guidance.

It is unnecessary to argue that for the Christian "What shall I do?" becomes "What wouldest thou have me to do?"; or that his faith involves the belief that God will and does reply to such a question. But to affirm this is not to suggest that a naïve acceptance of theism or a simple conviction that God answers prayer is sufficient to enable us to reach an inerrant decision. Indeed, in view of the claims lately made by the followers of Dr. Buchman, it is necessary to consider this matter in general before we can turn to our own particular example of it.

Few Christians will deny that in drawing attention to the need and possibility of an ordered life, to the duty and advantages of a quiet time and to the obligation of accepting, testing, and obeying what we receive as God's will, the Groups have reaffirmed a primary and universal Christian conviction. Every Church insists upon such discipline; and most of them make some provision both in public worship and in the training of their members for its performance. If it has fallen into neglect, this would certainly be a proof and a chief cause of spiritual failure.

At the same time it is only fair to observe that many of us have been seriously troubled both by the disclosures of psychologists as to the power of subconscious or latent motives, and by the verification in experience of the validity of their warnings. It is now a commonplace that in moments of quiet and deliberately trance-like receptivity we all become highly susceptible both to suggestions from others and to the uprush of repressed and unacknowledged desires. Prayer if it means merely the withdrawal of the consciousness from contact with its immediate surroundings and the cultivation of a state of passive contemplation renders us highly suggestible; and at such times voices may come to us with a startling sense of suddenness and objectivity—voices which subsequent reflection or a candid friend will convince us have their origin solely in our own psychic nature. Anyone who has lived among those Christians who find in prayer thus interpreted a constant means of settling difficulties will remember one instance after another of such error. Indeed, to make the subject a matter of prayer becomes with some of our friends an easy method not only of foreclosing an argument but of securing a victorious conclusion to it. For the answer is invariably in accordance with their expectations; and having obtained it they regard any further debate as contumacy and blasphemy.

It is, of course, far from my intention to decry the practice of prayer or to suggest that such a travesty of it is usual. But certainly in the methods of the Groups there seems a deliberate exposure of immature disciples to this kind of danger; and the instances of succumbing to it are unpleasantly frequent. Indeed, to ask a young and inexperienced person, worked up to a state of emotional tension, to keep a quiet time and to write down whatever ideas come into his mind during it would seem to be a short cut to the fostering of delusions. And even when the results have to be checked by standards of absolute honesty, purity, truth, and love, or by submission to the scrutiny of others, the method will hardly satisfy anyone who has passed beyond the most elementary stages of Christian life or has tried to formulate a coherently Christian philosophy.

To suppose that by merely abstracting ourselves from further intellectual or moral effort, when indeed no such effort has been seriously made, we can obtain guidance on issues of vast complexity and grave moral difficulty, is merely to revert to superstitious and magical concepts of God. We have learned to reject the idea of inspiration which represented the deity as taking control and dictating to his pythoness oracles which she repeated without understanding. Neither the writers of Scripture nor any other human being is an automaton; and God does not and will not treat them as such. At every level of religious aspiration man's response conditions God's revelation, distorting or enabling it according as heart and mind and will are in living communion with Him. Unless we have endeavoured not only to purify our emotions but to enlighten our minds and educate our wills, we cannot expect, we ought not to look for, guidance.

For in any truly incarnational philosophy worship involves not only adoration but consecration, not only contemplation but co-operation. The relationship is that of Creator and creature: but for the Christian it is also and supremely that of Father and child. "Henceforth I call you not slaves but I call you my friends; for the slave does not understand what his master is doing"* is a saying which reveals to us our privilege and our responsibility.

* John xv. 15.

THE PROBLEM OF GUIDANCE

If it be true, then communion with God demands not passivity, but an exercise of the personality at its fullest power, a concentration of all the faculties upon the task of loving, understanding, and serving; and prayer has nothing in common with trance or with auto-suggestion, and can only be undertaken in the effort to bring ourselves into a state of alertness and of preparation. To make guidance a substitute for thought, or to suppose that problems of conduct involving exact knowledge and a careful weighing of arguments can be settled without any qualification except the desire to be given a solution, is to misconceive the whole character of God's dealings with mankind. Religion, whatever its content, has never been a method of saving men from effort; and Christianity, whatever may be true of other religions, has always insisted upon the need for active and intelligent discipleship. To turn away from this world, ignoring its perplexities, stripping off its contacts, and swooning into the arms of the infinite, although it is a practice sanctioned by a few Christian mystics and devotees, is characteristic of the Buddha rather than the Christ; and is in the long run incompatible with any real faith in the Incarnation.

For in fact the notion which sets human understanding and divine guidance in contrast is not merely bad psychology (since the thinking self is an integral part of every normal human being), but is contrary to the facts. The effort to research into and discover the answer to the riddle of life is no less fitting a sphere for co-operation with God than is the effort to enter into quietness and listen for His voice. In science and philosophy not less than in art or in ethics the Spirit of God is active. We can "tune in" our minds as truly as our emotions; and if we are to yield ourselves to Him it will be our whole selves that He claims and can use. To discountenance the need for intellectual effort or to describe it as mere human arrogance is to lay aside the chief instrument by which we can be safeguarded against error. Human reason has its limitations and has often been accorded too exclusive a claim: but to refuse to use it to the uttermost and to prefer to it reliance upon emotions and intuitions is to leave ourselves at the mercy of our moods. Passive reliance upon guidance is a shirking of responsibility and a short cut which we have no right to take.

II

Christian prayer demands a much harder discipline. It signifies the attempt to bring into conscious relationship with God all the elements of life, to become sensitive to Him in and through all the contacts and activities of the self, to realize that nothing is apart from or indifferent to Him and that every lesser sphere should reveal and express His will. The life abundant which Christ came to bring is only a renunciation because it is a fulfilment. To attain it is not only or primarily to forsake all pride

THE PROBLEM OF GUIDANCE

and selfishness, but so to discover and accept the will of God that there is no longer room or desire for what is incompatible with His love. It is essentially a process not of escape but of sublimation.

So in this matter of the peace or war conflict, our search for guidance falls into two stages. Before we can begin to resolve it we must first study its character. In common with all such conflicts it presents itself to us as a choice of alternate modes of conduct between which the unitary individual must decide. More closely scrutinized it is discovered as a conflict within the self where forces are at work pulling towards or away from a particular course. We disclose in ourselves a clash of motives, and this inward battlefield is the sphere of decision. If we can settle the strife in our members, we shall thereby determine our line of action.

Before we can begin to do so, we must study the character of the issue—What is war? Why does it appeal to certain elements in me? Is that appeal valid? Are those elements sound? So too with peace—if I abstain, on what grounds shall I do so? Doing so, what is involved?

War obviously has its deepest roots in the will to live, in that struggle for existence which in one form or another plays and has played so large a part in evolution. Man, even in the twentieth century, inherits characteristic instincts of aggressiveness; as an individual he is impelled to assert his own independence; as a member of a group, family, class, or nation he carries over into his loyalty to it the same instincts of domination and pugnacity. That man is a fighting animal in the physical sense is in these days hardly true of the Western European. Blood lust or the condition vividly described as "seeing red" is not common among normal men and requires an intense emotional stimulus to awaken it. Military training makes almost no appeal to it: forming fours and shooting at a target are far more remote from it than a boxing match or a game of Rugby football: even sticking a bayonet into a sack is hardly more exciting than lashing at a golf ball. Indeed, athletics have served to satisfy man's urge towards physical combat—which is perhaps why war in 1914 had all the appearance of a great and dangerous game. Pugnacity played almost no part in the desire to enlist in 1914; nor did it loom large when the recruit found himself in the firing-line. One could find far more blood lust in professors and maiden ladies at home than in the soldiery at the front. Thwarted hate sets men ablaze: modern war has little in common with the berserk fury of earlier days.

Far more important as a motive was the desire to test out to the uttermost the quality of one's manhood. The same impulse sends men to Everest or the South Pole: it is the zest for adventure and achievement, the basic joy in exercising the faculties at their highest pitch. The desire to excel may have in it elements of competition; we would do what others cannot: or elements of fear, the simple fear of being afraid which led to many an act of seemingly

THE PROBLEM OF GUIDANCE

reckless gallantry. In 1914 the thought "here is the adventure that gives me my chance" was often stronger than the questions "so and so has gone, why not I?" and "is it fear that holds me back?"—though these were mixed up with it. War had always been regarded as the supreme proof of heroic worth: ordeal by battle was and is a significant phrase, which the present stress upon the bestiality of modern warfare will not wholly remove.

Individual instincts of self-assertion or of self-justification were of less effect in 1914 than those which control our relations with others. During the past century the individual has become increasingly conscious of his place in society, of his solidarity with his fellows, of his dependence upon corporate effort. If this is in most respects an advance, since fellowship is a nobler thing than egoism, it exposes us to the dangers of mob psychology, to propaganda, and mass madness. Few would deny that the normal man is less independent, and the abnormal more eccentric and self-conscious than in past generations. "Follow the band," whether from desire to keep faith or from dread of obloquy, was a recruiting agent of enormous power. Nationalism limited the majority to those who shared land and speech and government with us. We enlisted because king and country called us in tones and for reasons which we could not easily disobey.

For along with the desire to "do our bit" was a strong impulse of protective compassion. Whether or no Britain would have taken part in the war if

Belgium had not been invaded may well be doubted. But if the German thrust had been at Toul and Epinal instead of Liége and Namur, the emotional appeal against them would have lost most of its edge. No doubt to the more detached the smashing up of French forts and the shattering of French cities are no less damnable: but pity, in this nationalistic world, flows out to the individuals who compose a small people more readily than to those of a great Power. We might have argued for months over our obligation to defend France: the violation of Belgian neutrality, which we were pledged by treaty to defend, not only outraged our sense of duty but, appealing to our pity, solidified our will to fight in a day. To defend or avenge the weak is an instinct that goes deep. A man may legitimately refuse to fight for himself: it is difficult not to despise one who refuses to protect the oppressed by fighting—unless he can demonstrate that he is doing so by some more effective and more costly sacrifice.

What were the other influences that we could set against the pull of such powerful instincts? At first sight it is easy to say "self-preservation," the first and perhaps the strongest of all inherited motives. Most of us can recall cases in which physical fear or a selfishness which set its own survival before all other interests appeared to be the determinant factor: but we should admit that such were few, too few to give any sort of support to the theory that civilization has undermined the courage of the race. Certainly the scornful identification of conscientious objection with cowardice is an error of which those of us who accepted it would do well to repent. To face not only public denunciation but the reiterated assaults of tribunals, the loneliness and hardship of prison, and the reproach of friends called for conviction and fortitude of a singularly high quality.

For the mass of men it was not on instinctive grounds that the refusal to fight gained strength. Primitive instincts may be, as the psychologists tell us, still the driving-force of life: but, if so, they have been so long brought under the control of mental processes and constrained to find an outlet in directions sanctioned by thought that to most of us their primary and natural expression is no longer in any sense inevitable. Most of us recognizing the appeal of adventure, of loyalty, and of compassion could recognize that these might find satisfaction in resisting popular clamour, in obeying a higher than national loyalty, in extending our pity not only to the victims but to the agents of oppression. We could see that war threatened our hopes of human welfare, of international understanding, of social reform; that its outbreak was a manifestation of evil; that to take part in it, though this might be the best course under the circumstances, was yet to surrender the ideals which till then had claimed our allegiance.

Along with the destruction of our hopes for the world was all the business of killing. To enlist meant the willingness not only to lay down one's own life, but to destroy as our primary duty the lives of others. We might glorify the soldiers' calling and the dignity of death for the fatherland, but few of us had seen anything more violent than a college rag and could not picture ourselves engaged in bloodshed. War was no longer a matter of chivalry, of pitting one's valour against a rival, of charges and hand-to-hand encounters. If we could not foresee how impersonal and ruthless and unromantic it would become, at least it would be a strife of machines dealing death at a distance, machines whose end was the crushing of men like ourselves into a mush of torn and tortured flesh. The imaginative could not but realize the agony that it must involve, the heart-break which they must themselves strive to inflict. Was it possible for the sake of humanity to consent to anything so inhuman?

We might reply that there were occasions when homicide was justifiable; that to drive a bayonet into a man was a cleaner thing than to corrupt and dishonour him; that death and physical torment and the anguish of bereavement were less than the worst of evils: but such reasons could not easily justify us in inflicting them. Death is an irrevocable fact; and the command "Thou shalt do no murder" has therefore a peculiar urgency. There were times when war looked like nothing but mass murder.

Yet what else was to be done? Europe had chosen war. Our individual abstention could not affect that choice: indeed, it would only weaken the chance of a successful verdict for what was to us the more righteous cause. The triumph of the Central Powers would vindicate the claim that might is right; would enforce the belief in the appeal to arms; would enthrone the aggressors in a position of world supremacy. An Allied victory might mean an opportunity to make war impossible for the future; it would at least demonstrate the madness of militarism. An Allied defeat would destroy all hopes of peaceful progress; it would be the end of civilization as we knew it. This monstrous growth that threatened all that life meant to us must be treated with the knife: milder methods were powerless against the ethics of the jungle. Our country and all that it meant to us and to the world was in peril. If there were arguments against setting loyalty to it before loyalty to peace, they could be met by others which seemed to show that the only way to peace was war. Seen from the merely human standpoint such a conclusion might force itself upon us.

III

Such examination of the character of the decision is for the Christian only a preliminary. When he has traced out the factors of the conflict to their sources in his own nature, he can begin the more particular task of reviewing them in the light of his faith. He has set out the material for his choosing; now he must purge and sublimate and unify the self that is called to choose. For only as he brings himself to his own highest level of love and understanding and resolve can he claim to seek the issue from God. Indeed, the answer to his search will come as he consecrates himself to receive it.

It is with an act of will, an act of acknowledgment and submission, that worship begins. To fix the attention upon God, recalling whatever experience His name suggests and deliberately renewing the memory of that experience, is the first step. In the past we have had our moments of insight, moments that stand out as peaks in the level of our days and mark the opening up of new horizons. Following the road thus made clear to us we were accepting guidance and confirming our trust in our Guide: we were learning discipleship, the secret of which is not attainment but quest: we were "pressing on." There was a constraint upon us, the attraction of an end obscurely revealed and the support of a will which at times seemed manifestly other than our own. We were beginning to discover the meaning of "not my will, but thine, be done."

Recollecting such experiences it is easy to give meaning to the resolve to submit our own wills to God, to put ourselves into touch with Him, to arouse and enlarge our awareness of His nature and purpose. This is not to induce a state of quiescent suggestibility, the sort of trance which is too often and too easily produced by the repetition of familiar forms of worship. It is to respond with full and fixed consciousness to the *Sursum corda*. It is to bring all our powers to their highest attention, focusing the whole self upon its supreme source of integration. It is to enter into the presence of our manifested ideal—to be at once our own best self and caught up into communion with Him in whom that self is as nothing.

Then humbled and exalted, freed and controlled, we can bring our minds to play upon the issue that confronts us, letting the problem, piece by piece, take shape, and meditating upon it as it appears when studied under the aspect of the eternal. We shall then discern how much of our argument is specious and self-motived; how far pride and fear have influenced it; what of it can stand the test of our highest understanding of truth. What we have previously debated on the plane of bare intellect, now, brought into relation with a fuller experience and seen against a wider background, takes a new shape. If we cannot "think God's thoughts after Him," at least we can let our understanding of Him sift and test and arrange our argument.

In such effort there is attained a measure of detachment and of clarified and widened vision. The issues are seen in perspective—no longer from the selfish centre as they affect our own individual lives, but to some degree universally and in their bearing upon the general good. We escape from the dominance of the personal equation; and our judgment is freed from distractions and becomes steadier and more impartial. We catch a glimpse of the purpose and wholeness of our universe, and of our own lives and courses of action in relation to that wholeness. Instead of thinking only of our own path through the ups and downs of its career we become conscious of the movement around and embracing us, and can see ourselves as sharing in it and able to promote or impede its true direction.

In such an inquiry we can of course only discover what is true for us. Absolute truth is and must remain beyond us, and to claim that we can comprehend it or check our guidance by it is to confuse the Creator with the creature. Hence it by no means follows that a judgment valid for me is necessarily valid for another. If after trying to think out the problem of peace or war *sub specie eternitatis*, I reach a clear conviction, I may put the case as I have come to see it before others, but must not be shocked or censorious if they after equally honest enquiry disagree with me. To assume that God's will for me, even if I am confident of its intention, is universally binding, is an act of arrogance. To be freed from my own self-will is to discover a penitent reverence for the personalities of others. To condemn is to be condemned.

For the phase of intellectual effort passes into the final stage of our quest. As the mind is released from its egoisms, the emotions are purged alike from bitterness and from sentimentality: to understand is to sympathize: truth and love, so often at variance within us, can now disclose their unity. It is when understanding is thus quickened into love that our worship rises to its fulfilment: it is at such moments that God can speak to us or in us. We are attuned to Him. Our attention sensitive over the whole range of its experience becomes focused upon Him as the unifying and creative reality of the universe. We pass from adoration of the all-pervading to adoration of the alone, from God as manifested in His works to God as we can begin to conceive Him in Himself. For some all other revelations find their consummation in the Christ: for some there may come an instant when even that supreme sacrament is transcended.

In such moments a constraint is laid upon the worshipper. He returns an integrated personality and knows what alone he must do.

IV

It has been necessary to set out with some fulness what the attempt to reach a Christian solution involves, because there is much talk both about guidance and about prayer which would represent them as light tasks followed by magical results. Most of us have heard too much of trivial answers to prayer or of guidance which is obviously shallow and wrong-headed: most of us recognize how readily our own repressed desires can burst upon the consciousness and assume the aspect of a voice from heaven. In view of such experiences we dare not suggest that the Christian's duty of seeking the will of God is to be easily or unadvisedly fulfilled. Prayer is a mockery unless it involves effort.

Guidance can only be sought if we are willing to fit ourselves for it.

Even so, it is only according to the measure of our knowledge of God that we can learn His will for us; only as our love of Him is pure that He can guide us rightly. In this matter of peace or war, in any of the graver conflicts that we would resolve, we can only go step by step. As we go, fresh experience will demand a revision of our judgment. No problem is ever finally solved. What was true and right for me in 1914 need not therefore be my course to-day; nor in recalling the division of opinion when the war broke out shall I easily denounce one or the other choice as atheistic. It is indeed certain that many of those who decided differently then did so after full consideration and an agony of worshipful effort, and that many of them if faced with the same issue now would be likely to reverse their decision.

Yet this is not to say that the problem of right conduct in 1914 was only soluble on a purely individual basis. Certain clear convictions on matters of principle emerged from any honest search for guidance. Questions remained on which each of us could only pronounce with hesitation: but they were not the questions usually supposed to be crucial.

Few British citizens could really study the matter from a Christian standpoint without concluding that the current assertions both of pacifists and militarists were fallacies. "Christ or Caesar" when Christ meant prison and Caesar the trenches is almost as grotesque an exaggeration as "My country right or wrong," though it is of course far less immoral. None who realize the supreme place that fellowship plays in the life of man can dismiss the duty of citizenship as a merely secular allegiance. In the family, the state, the nation, mankind has slowly risen from an individual towards a fully personal existence. Through the creative power of social activities he has won, partially and incompletely, all that releases him from a brutish egotism. The discipline of mutual obligation, the partnership in ever-widening endeavour, are indispensable stages in education for the Kingdom of God: if they foreshadow a fellowship not yet attained, it is only as we learn what they can teach that we can prepare ourselves for that fellowship. Rightly regarded Church and State are alike training grounds in corporate living, bodies in and through which the body of Christ is being prepared. To cut the two asunder as if one were wholly His and the other an obvious Antichrist is a false simplification. It is a revival of the outworn belief that secular and sacred are radically disparate and easily segregated. In both spheres as in all His creation the Spirit of God works; and if in the Church the consciousness of His presence and the provision of manifold opportunities for His activity enable a vastly richer development of life in Him, yet He is not on that account foreclosed from other and effective ranges of operation. Whatever are the faults and shames of Britain we owe too much to our earthly citizenship to set it in bare contrast with our loyalty to Christ. If in a crisis we are called to renounce obedience to the will of our countryman, we must see to it that our love for the ordered community is not less deep than that of those who die for it.

Such love is of course travestied when it accepts the blind blasphemy of "My country right or wrong." Love, though it may find joy in the faults of the beloved, will not, at its best, ignore or acquiesce in them—otherwise it degenerates into sentimentality. Love, despite the moderns, cannot be indifferent to moral worth, and if it is to deserve its name must strive passionately and austerely for the highest welfare of its object. The Christian whose primary allegiance is to Him in whom is "neither Greek nor Jew" has at once a standard by which to estimate his nation's value and an ideal which that nation must serve. Only as Britain becomes Christ-like, only as nationalism evidently contributes to universal life in Christ, can he be content to give to it his full affection and service. To assume that British supremacy is necessarily God's will, to claim to be His "chosen people," to insist that we can serve Him better by victory than by martyrdom is to reveal a tragic ignorance of Christ. That such ideas can still exist among Christians shows how deeply the influence of the more primitive parts of the Old Testament has obscured both the teaching of the great prophets and the significance of Christ crucified.

It should not be necessary to expand so obvious

THE PROBLEM OF GUIDANCE

a truism. But the rise of the "British Israel" heresy in our own country—a heresy at least as serious and unintelligible as the outbursts of extreme "German Christians"—is proof of the extent of such errors. Precious as is our heritage of Old Testament scriptures its influence, thanks to doctrines of verbal inspiration and to concentration in childhood upon the less edifying parts of the historical books, has often been deplorable. Ideas of a tribal God and a chosen people, of the Lord as a man of war and the brigand chief as His favourite instrument, of material prosperity as the reward of His approval and calamity as evidence of His displeasure, are appropriate enough to the earlier stages of man's quest for God: they are already transcended in the nobler portions of the Old Testament, but are the chief cause of the rejection of Jesus and the persecution of His followers in the New. They are stages, early stages, in religious history which Christ wholly superseded and to which His disciples cannot relapse without apostasy.

The clash of opposing loyalties could thus for most Christians be readily resolved: to Christ, first and last, their faith must hold: His will must be theirs, whether they saw that will as best served by espousing or renouncing the nation's cause. The conflict for them ceased to be one between opposing ends, and was confined to the further question of the means by which His will could be faithfully maintained. Was it possible, now or ever, to regard the State as an instrument of His will? Was it in keeping with His example to use physical force in the struggle of life? Was it true that war, reinforcing His practice of living dangerously, fostered qualities of supreme value? There were some who believed that any method that involved armed resistance was thereby forbidden to the Christian: there were others who pointed to battle as the finest training-ground of heroic virtue. Each of these alternatives is itself an over-simplification: but each raises wide and difficult issues that cannot be dismissed without full discussion. It is in the attempt to resolve them that the chief problems of our enquiry arise.

CHAPTER IV

THE CHRISTIAN AND THE STATE

I

It has already been argued that for most of the citizens of Great Britain the sharp distinction between Christ and Caesar was an impossible simplification. In view both of the facts of history and experience, and also of a sound philosophy of the relation between the individual and society, the doctrine of the non-moral State and, therefore, of the radical difference between personal and collective ethics is one which most Englishmen would immediately reject. As such, in considering the clash of loyalties in 1914, it was sufficient to dismiss it in a paragraph; for it was, in fact, so dismissed by the vast majority of us. Indeed, the conviction that the same moral and religious standards must guide both private and national conduct is so fundamental to our whole habit of mind that it comes as a shock to realize that this belief is by no means universal. When certain German apologists for war proclaimed that Christianity, though the mainspring of individual piety and well-being, could not be applied to civic activities, we regarded their plea as a piece of Satanic special pleading. When we find American Christians drawing a sharp line between the functions of the civic and of the religious communities and condemning the former as necessarily secular and essentially non-moral, we experience a surprise almost amounting to revulsion. Yet such views are, in fact, still so widely held that if we are to examine the question of pacifism with any completeness they cannot be summarily dismissed. For not only do they affect our attitude towards every sort of corporate problem, but they give rise to two distinct and contrasted positions. Some in accepting them argue as Tolstoy did, that for the Christian total renunciation of civic responsibility is the only consistent course; others, as different in most respects as General Bernhardi and Professor Reinhold Niebuhr,* agree that if personal and national ethics are thus disparate the Christian can legitimately follow one set of principles as an individual and another as a citizen.

To illustrate the importance of a decision on this issue a reminiscence drawn from a different field of social activity may be appropriate. Until I was sent out to the International Missionary Council at Jerusalem to discuss religious education, it had hardly occurred to me that any Christian could regard the provision of a purely secular system by the State as anything but a deplorable consequence of the disunion of the Churches. Certainly I had never met any Christian in Britain who would

* His dictum that "human collectives are less moral than the individuals which compose them" is one that I have examined at length in my *Creator Spirit*, pp. 169–203. Both psychology and history seem to me to disprove its universal validity. It is of course manifestly sub-Christian in its view of human nature.

advocate it or be willing to accept it except as a "second best." Yet I found that my American colleagues not only treated the non-interference of the State with religion as axiomatic, but could hardly be convinced that there was any objection or any alternative to a rigid dualism. When I urged that the British delegation would certainly refuse any solution which secularized the State, and argued that if we stood by our belief that religion was the essential basis of any sound education we could not condemn the State to provide something radically defective; they listened to me with the greatest generosity and gave full weight in their Report to my convictions. But it was evident that in so doing they sacrificed if not a principle at least a deep-seated habit of mind.

The defence of this contrast between Church and State seems to depend upon the three following arguments: that Jesus and the New Testament generally confine attention to personal religion, and contemplate the development of the Christian way within the framework of a secular system indifferent or even hostile; that when the Church in the course of its growth began to intervene in imperial politics it fatally compromised its own primary loyalty and fell away into worldliness; that, since the attempt at an ecclesiastical theocracy has plainly demonstrated the futility of such dreams, the State has not been and perhaps cannot be ordered upon the principles of the Gospel. As a consequence the Christian must recognize that he lives in two worlds and must adjust his conduct to two conflicting spheres of obligation.

II

That the religion of the New Testament is a Word of God utterly alien from and condemnatory of all merely human policies is a conviction that has lately been expressed in uncompromising fashion by Dr. Barth and his followers. In their denunciation of the humanistic and, as they would urge, frankly infidel optimisms of Liberal Protestantism and the so-called "Social Gospel" the Barthians are to some extent reflecting the post-war despair. That man-made civilisation is in any case insecure, that our present culture is doomed, that our arrogant self-confidence and godless faith in the inevitable progress of scientific efficiency is a flat denial of the essential quality of any true religion, are conclusions to which the post-war world, especially in Germany, easily turn. The school in adopting such an attitude is in part the product of contemporary circumstances. In part it provides a true criticism of them. To dismiss it as a mere reaction against a discredited humanism is unjust; for Dr. Barth in reaffirming the transcendentalism and otherness of God has done more than protest against identifying social welfare with spiritual development. He has recalled Christians to their primary concern, has reasserted the necessity of penitence, of conversion, of dependence, and has warned us that the disciples of the

Crucified may not identify worldly success with religious achievement or fail to meet the wisdom of this world with a sharp challenge.

To admit that modern humanism and even certain exponents of social Christianity deserve the Barthian censure and should accept its call to repentance, is not to justify the Barthian separation between sacred and secular, or to suggest that Barth's theology has any constructive value. It is, in fact, just the counterpart of the Liberal Protestantism which it attacks. Both of them start from the premiss that religion is a matter of individual piety, even when, like Ritschl, they react against it: both accept the contrast between secular activities and the culture of individual salvation: both of them fail to develop any true sacramental or incarnational theology. In Christology the Liberals tend to become Adoptionists—their Christ is the peasant-prophet, the greatest of the sons of men—and in their doctrine of God immanentists for whom adoration in the Catholic sense is an unknown quality. The Barthians are exactly the opposite: their Christ is a divine intruder and their God an external and transcendent deity: they can give no meaning to the Holy Spirit, and no sense to the Pauline claim that man is a co-operator with God. Neither party has ever understood the position which British theology during the past century has been concerned to maintain, that while God and man are essentially distinct as Creator and creature, or as Spirit and flesh, yet that the union of the two in the one Christ involves the belief that they have been, can be, and ultimately must be united; that there is no radical antithesis between God and the world; and that only as the creature sacramentally manifests the Creator, responding to and expressing the energy of His Spirit, can the divine purpose be fulfilled. With us, ever since Fox and the early Quakers, or, in the Church of England, since F. D. Maurice, it has been clear that individual salvation and social redemption could not be set in contrast; that the Christian must work to bring all life within the rule of Christ; that, as Dr. Oman* has put it, "reconciliation to the evanescent is revelation of the eternal." No doubt to attain this end there is need to assert both the otherness of God and the responsibility of man; no doubt such a dual assertion is ultimately a paradox: but any theology, whether Liberal Protestant, or Barthian, which would resolve the paradox by denying one element in it stands condemned on theological grounds as irreconcilable with a true faith in Incarnation.

Lest this be thought a mere insular prejudice, it should be added that despite their monumental achievements in the realm of scholarship, their industry and ingenuity, German theologians have, in fact, failed to develop any such treatment of the scope and implications of Christianity as has become general in Britain. The experience of anyone who has taken part in international conferences like the Life and Work Conference at Stockholm in 1924

* *The Natural and the Supernatural*, p. 470.

will bear out the conclusion that our Churches are at least a generation (some would say a century) ahead of those of Central Europe in their grasp of the social implications of the Gospel. Nor should we admit for an instant that this was due to any "synkretismus" or secularizing of our religion: on the contrary we should claim to have a stronger sense of worship both private and public, and a truer sacramentalism. Far as we are from any worthy expression of our Christianity in our corporate life, we shall do disservice if we too modestly accept Dr. Barth's strictures as applicable to us, or his position as anything more than a valuable but illogical and incoherent protest. If he had worked in a sphere where secular and sacred were not so rigidly discriminated, or where there was a stronger combination of worship and social service, his outlook would not have been what it is. We owe so much in biblical, historical, and critical studies to the labours of German scholars that it is necessary in all seriousness to point out that in doctrinal theology, and especially in the problems that surround the relation of the individual to the community, we shall be guilty of a seriously retrograde step if we deny our own tradition at the bidding of their latest representative.

For indeed this tradition, far more than his dogmatic, is true to the religion of the New Testament and to the main stream of Christian development. That Jesus insisted upon the primacy of God and the absolute claim of God's Kingdom, is common ground to us and to him. Worship as the proper response of the creature to the Creator, loving obedience as of children to the Father, readiness to gain at whatever cost the pearl of great price —that is the essence of the Gospel. But such a relationship to God involves inevitably a corresponding relationship of love and service to humanity, and of wonder and acceptance towards nature. If God is what Christ reveals, then there is nothing outside His care and ultimate control; no sphere which can be impervious to His influence; no activity unrelated to His will. To serve Him is to labour always and everywhere that that will may be done as in heaven so on earth: it is to learn that nothing is common or unclean: it is to see the evidence of His presence in the attainment by humanity of that fulness of life which Christ foretold for those who sought first His Kingdom and righteousness.

Nor, for many of us, is it possible if we accept the incarnational principle, to regard the natural order as only the scene or theatre in which the divine drama of redemption is played out. Though Jesus is unique, yet His uniqueness is, as the New Testament constantly insists, that of the first fruits; His relation to the Father is symbolic of what is already existent in its appropriate degree throughout the Universe, and prophetic of the day when God shall be all in all. Immanentism, though it easily degenerates into an unethical and non-theistic pantheism, is implied by faith in the unity of God and man in Christ and explicit in the Church's belief in the Holy Spirit. As such it vindicates our insistence that the line between sacred and secular cannot be sharply drawn, that the Universe derives its value from the manifestation of deity within it, and that where love, joy, and peace, the fruit of the Spirit, are revealed in men, there and to that extent they are evidently the sons of God.

III

This plainly does not mean that there is no room for distinctions of degree, or indeed, for contrasts so strong that the passage from one to the other is a change from death to life. If all are within the purpose and operation of God, yet the extent to which they can reveal or co-operate with Him varies over the widest range. It is doubtless true that

"I but open my eyes and perfection, no more and no less,
  In the kind I imagined confronts me, and God is seen God
  In the stone, in the star, in the flesh, in the soul, and the clod."

But the "kinds" differ vastly; and to form an image of the divine after a pattern lower than the highest is idolatry.

This is notably the case when the insufficiency of the creature is intensified by its rebellion. Sin, the frustration of God's purpose, the perversion of His instruments to baser uses, is a fact of which no sensitive observer can be unaware. In himself and in his world he finds a huge discrepancy between what might be and what is, between the man or woman whom he knows and the child of God of whom he dreams, between the jungle warfare of human society and the fellowship of which he would believe it to be capable. At his best and in moments of adoration he can so far escape from his prison of pride and individuality as to experience communion with the eternal, forgiveness and admission into the community of the re-born—an experience sufficient to reveal to him a mode of being that satisfies the restlessness of his soul and gives him at last a home. But such glimpses, however he may strive to fix them, if they disclose haunting and splendid possibilities, throw into deeper contrast the realm of egoism from which he cannot wholly escape, and in which he is for the most part content to live. Child of the heavenlies or child of earth—which is his true nature? which the reality and which the illusion?

Here is his two-fold status: here the basis of his life's conflict: here the perpetual crisis under which he is arraigned. It is the dualism thus created, the consequent succession of choices, the aspirations and agonies that give its meaning to man's existence and its vital element to his religion. To those sensitive to the issues at stake, the passion in the soul of a St. Paul, the catastrophic drama of Apocalyptic, the visions of paradise and hell, seem no longer exaggerated or unreal. It is by them that the only significant issue is depicted: it is in their language

THE CHRISTIAN AND THE STATE

that the alternative presents itself. God or Satan, Christ or Mammon, the Church and the World, the saved and the damned, such antitheses stand out clear-cut and vivid; and between them each of us must choose.

The history of religions reveals the varied forms in which that choice has been made. To cultivate the spirit or to mortify the flesh, to discipline the will by conscious effort or to surrender its control to a master-loyalty, to renounce the world or to labour for its betterment—all such methods have been commended within the Christian tradition. Each of them has its representatives in the religions of mankind. Ultimately the modes of conduct thus displayed derive their character from the creeds of which they are the expression. Theology should determine ethics. But however clear the concept of God it is no easy business to conform practice to principle. And in periods like the present, when the general outlook upon the Universe is changing rapidly, anomalies are obvious and perhaps inevitable.

Yet for the Christian, and despite elements in the history of Christendom that challenge such a verdict, certain convictions seem plain. For him there can be no ultimate dualism. God is Creator, and the world is in His control. To restrict God's activity within it to particular covenanted spheres is to impose on Him limits which we do not possess the knowledge to define. To cut ourselves off from any part of it as irredeemably evil is to betray our calling. To serve, that by every means and in all relations God's will may be done, is the purpose of discipleship. To begin such service from the conviction that all things are of God, that evil, however flagrant, can be made to yield, that it is our task to appeal to the best in men rather than to denounce the worst, these are plain lessons of Christ. To identify oneself with the rebels while refusing to countenance their rebellion, to minister to their needs even at the cost of utter loneliness and self-abnegation, to take up a cross and be crucified by those whom He comes to save—that is Christ's way and His disciples are those who follow it.

For His method consistently with His concept of God's nature and purpose is to demand a wholeness of consecration which cannot be identified with a particular programme of detailed reforms. Men must change not their opinions only but the central motive and direction of their lives. He sets before men an absolute and, seeing what they are, unattainable standard; and though He will illustrate its application in regard to special issues, love of enemies, truthfulness, sexual fidelity, and the like, He will not let them suppose that obedience in these respects exhausts their obligation or that the art of living in the Spirit can be fulfilled by observance of moral precepts.* Herein He differs from all previous teachers, from John the Baptist and the

---

* Cf. Brunner, *The Mediator*, p. 420: "The Sermon on the Mount has no gaps because it gives no instructions. It gives isolated examples of the one Good, the absolute Good, the Impossible."

Prophets. They are content to denounce special evils and exhort to special acts of penitence: He demands not betterment but the best. He bids men seek God's Kingdom and righteousness; for as they do so they will cease to hate and lie and lust, and will do so without self-righteousness. Nowadays as of old we prefer programmes, and are inclined to apologize for His failure to supply them, and to take upon ourselves to supply the defect.

This is a point which if it be true goes deep. His method involves the conviction that as men become aware of God and are caught by the passion for Him they will in fact find that their whole attitude towards their fellows and the world is transformed. They will no longer have the pride which expresses itself in sin or the insensitiveness which is blind to corporate evil. They will bring a leaven of health into a diseased society; they will deal not with the symptoms but with the cause of corruption; they will reveal a new way of life which men will recognize and desire and welcome and eventually fulfil.

IV

Does this mean that Christ presents to men an ideal of perfection which in fact is only attainable by a sort of miracle—a miracle which He may have expected to happen apocalyptically, but which in fact has not been and cannot be fulfilled? If we are to insist that the wholeness of the Gospel cannot be analysed or codified, cannot be presented in terms of step by step attainment, cannot be identified with any special issue without losing its essential quality, must we not then regard Christian history as a shameful betrayal and the good news itself as a mocking vision?

To do so would be to ignore Christ's infinite tenderness towards His manifestly imperfect followers, His quickness to recognize and commend their first faltering steps towards discipleship, His trust that even by such instruments the Kingdom can be proclaimed and established. He claims perfection—no less: otherwise we should not be unprofitable servants and could bargain with His demands. But while claiming it, He shows an infinite patience with the blindness and waywardness, the fears and egoisms of His people. As He was content to lead bit by bit along the road, so surely He would commend to us an attitude which at once insists uncompromisingly upon the fulness of the end to be attained, and recognizes joyfully each little stage towards its attainment. There must be no exclusiveness; nothing human lies outside the Spirit's transforming power: no complacency; we have not attained save as we press on to a goal still far away: no despair; for love is sovereign, and its crucifixion is not a tragedy but a triumph.

It is so easy, in view of the demands of the Gospel, to condemn the Church, as does Dr. Cadoux, for its concession in the matter of military service—thereby saying in effect "pacifism is the essence of Christianity: to abandon it was an apostasy." To do so is surely to suggest that Christ came to give a code of rules and that the Church can be judged by its failure to observe them—which is the same error as that which would identify Christianity with the Nicene Creed, and denounce those who cannot accept it as excluded from the way. It may well be that the Churchmen who accepted Constantine as a Christian without insisting that he renounce his throne or disband his legions were choosing a less than perfect course—even as it may be that the anathema was a less than Christian instrument against the Arians. Such judgments are natural and perhaps just: none of us is without sin: but it is doubtful if denunciation of the error from us who are in fact all under the same condemnation serves any very clearly Christian end. If the Church had not come to terms with the Empire, if Christendom had not been institutionalized, if at this or that crisis other counsels had prevailed—such speculations have a strong but unprofitable fascination. They resemble the questionings of those who cavil at certain elements in the natural order, who would have a world without earthquakes, an evolution without the liver-fluke or the praying mantis or the tiger, a humanity without cancer or insanity. We can of course deny the morality of the Creator because of such apparent blots upon His work, even as we can deny His operation in history because its record is full of inconsistencies and retrogressions. But ultimately if both space and time, both the Universe and its story are sacramental—and this is surely the only conclusion for the theist—we must accept their imperfections as within God's purpose, and concern ourselves not with indicting the past but with resolving to benefit by its lessons and not repeat its errors.

For myself, at least, it seems plain that along with the insistence upon the highest and a constant protest on behalf of perfectionism, we must be content to recognize a step-by-step development and to excuse, in others though not in ourselves, the inevitable concessions which we make when we accept the best possible under the circumstances. And when it is argued that to degrade the conditions of Church membership so as to permit the baptism of the heathen empire on easy terms was not the best possible, then I can only acknowledge that though to-day I should condemn the setting up of a double standard whereby certain Christians were encouraged to seek the anchorite's cell or the coenobite's cloister while others were suffered to follow secular careers in a secular spirit, I cannot be so sure of my right to condemn the Church of the fourth century. For after all it was precisely this policy which enabled her to survive the barbarian invasions and to preserve at whatever cost the substance of the faith. If further I am told that to justify compromise then is to encourage it in the same field to-day, the reply is easy. I may be uncertain of the measure of condemnation appropriate to the Church of the fourth century when she relaxed her pacifism: I shall not on that account hesitate to insist that now when a similar issue presents itself the Church must re-examine the position, and, in my judgment, should reach a totally different decision. That is the only way in which I can interpret the mind of Him who clearly laid down the principles of brotherhood and yet did not insist upon an immediate liberation of slaves, of Him who is justly called the Prince of Peace though He never denounced war or refused the friendship of its soldiers.

V

Thus to combine a strong and worshipful consciousness of perfection and an infinite patience with the manifestly imperfect aspirations of mankind is of course extraordinarily hard. How are we to keep our sense of God and of the unattainable demand of the eternal clear and whole, while at the same time we are striving in every circumstance of our many-sided endeavours to advance a tiny step out of the "mire and clay"? Idealist and realist, visionary and man of affairs, dreamer whose dreams come true—that is the Christian's calling, and it follows a narrow road. We have to live up to and strive to extend our sense of obligation, so that our loyalty may be concrete and uncompromising. And we have to do so when every contact with the world involves a threat of compromise and the pain of unfulfilled desires.

There are, as we know, some rare souls so haunted

by perfection that the cruel business of enduring the second best becomes intolerable for them. We have all known moments when the mass of iniquity around and within breaks in upon us and we feel the burden of this death, the savour of corruption, defiling every sanctity of our souls. At such times, were it not for the example of the Christ, we should feel that clean and wholesome life was on earth utterly unattainable: at such moments we get nearest to an understanding of His passion.

In them it is hopeless to make confession of particular sins or to console ourselves with the belief that in this direction or that we have some trifling cause for satisfaction. We cannot isolate one source of evil and concentrate upon it. We see the horror of war and the urgency of the task of reconciliation: but we cannot discriminate between the strife of nations and the strife of sects or firms or families. Indeed, we feel that to direct attention to one field of endeavour will only involve us in acquiescence in others, that to cast out one demon (even if by a lifetime of devotion we can do so) is either to ignore all the others, or to give the impression that duty can be defined as the discharge of a successive number of such efforts, or to suggest that health consists not in wholeness but in the removal one by one of diseases. We can, I think, see in our Lord's own hesitation in working His cures His sense of the danger of allowing His ministry to become thus specialized. We can, I am sure, see how such a policy leads to a loss of perspective, to an unwholesome fanaticism, and to a morbid outlook in those who follow it.

Yet when the vital importance of this sense of perfection and of the consequent sense of guilt is recognized, it remains true that neither Jesus nor His greatest disciples have given way to it. They have shown us that the most overwhelming conviction of the reality and holiness of God can be combined with an infinite compassion and trust and perseverance in dealing with the horror of iniquity. At such moments we are liable to feel that life is unendurable, and to be driven into martyrdom or an asylum as a refuge from its contaminating touch. Yet Jesus is content to go on His way working to-day and to-morrow until the time of His glorification is complete, and the issue on which He will stake His life has arisen. And St. Paul, though realizing that to go away and be with Christ is far the best, is ready to labour incessantly over the petty problems, the lapses and renewals, of his converts. The great Christians have always been realists, serenely practical over small things, never despairing because the task was great and the progress slow and the end not yet: or rather they have been great artists cherishing the eternal beauty and yearning to give it expression in the earthly medium of their craft.

When we look into their experience we see that it is just the quality of their faith that enables them so to reconcile the incompatibles. For us desire and performance, God and human affairs, are hopelessly estranged. We despair of bringing vision to achievement; and rightly despair. But for those who have entered more deeply into the experience of religion the contrast seems to be resolved. The same faith which emphasizes the awful holiness and otherness of God emphasizes also His unending and illimitable energies, His amazing and unmerited love. In consequence the sense of corruption never becomes dominant: sin is never in the forefront: nothing, not even the stubborn iniquity of man, is outside the Father's care and resources. Love wins—at the price of the Cross.

So they can go forward never despairing, working out from day to day the constraints of faith and dealing with each situation as it arises. The infinity of their resourcefulness is not less amazing than the patience and consistency of their endeavours. It may be what we reckon a great issue: it may be something relatively trivial. They deal with all alike in the same Spirit, content to go from one to another as occasion arises, and to find in them all a way for the realizing of their dreams. There is nothing formal or cut and dried about diagnosis or treatment: every case is handled on its merits and on the plane of personal relationships: and each illustrates a fresh application of the same unchanging principles. Nor is there anything hectic or neurotic about their methods. They deal with difficulties and errors that have actually arisen on lines which as applied in other directions will make for health: but they do not refuse to give the half-loaf because the recipient is not yet capable of absorbing the whole. It is as if, just because they knew the grandeur and remoteness of the goal, they could be enormously patient in enabling small concrete approximations towards it. They are content to help the children of God to crawl before they can walk, and to walk before they can fly. Too many of us are only willing to say "either wings or immobility, either a full meal or starvation."

At first sight this may seem like a deliberate acceptance of an empirical and compromising programme. We are apt to identify the best possible under the circumstances with the second best, and this with a refusal of the good. Why did not Christ tell the centurion that his calling was so evil that he must resign it before help could be given him? Why did not St. Paul denounce slavery instead of merely reminding the master that his slave was also his brother? Such questions obtrude themselves and cannot lightly be dismissed. For they bear inevitably upon any such problem as that which we are now discussing, and can be used to foreclose any effort to extend the scope of discipleship. How was it that a demand for perfection could be combined with such significant silences? Is it necessary in aiming high deliberately to weaken the demand until its fulfilment is brought within reach?

VI

There is one obvious and widely given answer which must be considered sympathetically, though for many of us it is wholly unsatisfying. The Catholic tradition in moral theology has laid down a clear distinction between the works of perfection and the obligatory duties of the secular Christian. To divide acts of sin into mortal and venial, to lay down a definite minimum of religious observances, and to insist that while every disciple must reach this easy standard none must be constrained and most must be discouraged if they wish to exceed it, is a simple and practicable method. It secures that certain definite evils can be suppressed, that the world's work can be carried on without undue disturbance, and that contentment and obedience can be considered a sufficient qualification for spiritual safety. Yet it enables those who display clear aptitude for further endeavour to press on towards full saintliness: it produces a strong and simple discipline and a vigorous corporate life: and it combines idealism, the maintenance of a clear standard of Christian perfection, with realism, the adaptation of the ideal to the practical necessities and varying capabilities of the average sensual man.

No one who has studied the content or learned to appreciate the achievements of Catholic Moral Theology will fail to recognize the power of its appeal. Administered by a priesthood trained in the exercise of the penitential system it has moulded a multitude of individuals of all ages and races and has shaped more evidently than any other influence the character of European ethics. Its precision and coherence, if they do not justify the frequent claim to constitute Christian civilization, at least form an impressive contrast with the hesitant and often unstable demands of non-Roman Christendom. Here is a great code of Torah, tested by centuries of experience, appropriate to the vagaries of human temperament and the varieties of human circumstance, and enabling those who accept it to find relief from the stress of private decisions, from the fret of conscience and the peril of indifference. Those of us who are aware of the swing to and fro between moods of bewildered aspiration and of helpless acquiescence must often have longed to surrender our responsibilities into the hands of authority. Probably it is to its moral discipline even more than to its doctrinal clarity that the Church of Rome owes its attraction.

Yet, when its appeal is fully admitted, there remains a conviction that so simple a solution of our dilemma is wholly unacceptable; and such a conviction is based upon principles which go deep into our whole concept of the religion of Christ and its revelation of God and His dealings with mankind. Our objection to it is not based upon the abuses of the confessional, or upon the defects of the code, or upon the failure of Catholicism to inspire and guide progress—though all these are true enough. The underlying grounds of protest are more profound.

Historically it was the Pauline doctrine of grace which produced the revolt against mediaeval orthodoxy. The Catholic system was and is a Law. What the Scribes of the Pharisees had done for Moses that the doctors of the Church had done for Christ. Texts of the New Testament had been transformed into a new decalogue. Virtues and vices had been classified and defined. Elaborations, works of obligation, and works of supererogation, had been devised. A vast corpus of ecclesiastical jurisprudence and legalized ethics had been created. Grace had ceased to be a gracious personal relationship and had become a mechanically earned reward consequent upon the performance of specified duties. St. Paul, who knew well the value of the Law as a schoolmaster to bring men to Christ and had grown up under a similar system, lived and strove in vain if the religion of freedom was to be replaced in Christ's name by a return to legal tutelage.

The teaching of Jesus is radically opposed to such an ethic. We are unprofitable servants; and when any man can say "I am in a state of salvation," his spiritual condition is that of the Pharisee in the parable. Here is the defect in all theories which substitute duty for love: they cut the hamstring of spiritual aspiration; they replace the infinite demands of personal attachment by a series of concrete and dischargeable obligations. Obedience often masquerades as humility: it belongs to a lower ethical category. Christians, be they popes or charcoal-burners, are "called to be saints," and their vocation cannot be reduced to the discharge of works of necessity. It may be legitimate in a University to institute a double standard; and to bestow the same degree upon Pass and Honours candidates alike. The result in the Catholic Church has been to separate the secular from the religious, the natural from the supernatural; to offer to the average man a list of relatively simple tasks which kills in him his native thirst for perfection—that divine discontent which is the spring of religious achievement; and to secure discipline at the cost of destroying adventure. "I press on," is the enemy of "I have attained."

That Catholic Moral Theology has thus become legalistic is clearly seen by its failure to adjust itself to the widening demands of human idealism. Our Lord's parable of the patch of new cloth on the old garment draws attention to the inevitable failure of such systems. Law is valuable, so long as it remains consistent and unchanging. To patch upon the Torah His new freedom in the matter of fasting would be to rend the old robe irreparably. So to-day, when changed circumstances and the increase of knowledge have effected large changes in our ethical outlook, Catholics find themselves committed to positions which shock the sensitive conscience. To make concessions is to admit the inadequacy of the system and to nullify its claim to unquestioning obedience: yet to persist in advocating anachronisms is to invite a slower but not less fatal collapse. Anyone who watches the efforts of Catholic tradition to adapt an obsolescent philosophy of sex to the conscience of to-day will feel that a system so demonstrably obscurantist can hardly maintain its status as Christian.

There is of course a simple proof of the radical difference between legalism and Christianity. "Hard cases make bad law" is a sound maxim for the jurist. Individuals must be treated in the light of statutes, of generalizations appropriate perhaps to an average, and at their best devised for the protection of society. But Christ always refused to generalize. He treated each individual as a person with his own particular circumstances and needs. He never fell back upon maxims or stretched His penitents upon a bed of Procrustes. To Him as to Christianity every case is a hard case: we are all "prodigal children," sons of God and miserable sinners; and there is no broad highway for the fulfilment of love's wayfaring. Those who remember Mr. Geoffrey Studdert-Kennedy's pathetic novel, *I Pronounce Them*, will realize how impossible a wise and sensitive Christian prophet found it to reconcile his Christian love with the observance of the tradition: when I asked him if he really accepted the solution given in his book and could have deliberately wrecked two human lives in order to conform to the law, I shall not soon forget his emphatic protest against such a course. In the abstract he advocated Catholicism, in practice his conscience revolted against it.

The rigidity of the orthodox Moral Theology and its inadequacy in the light of modern aspiration is as clear in the matter of war as in the field to

THE CHRISTIAN AND THE STATE 119

which we have referred. It may or may not have been necessary for the Church to abandon its early opposition to the bearing of arms. The case for pacifism to-day need not conflict with the belief that such a concession was the best possible under the circumstances. But to rivet upon modern Christians St. Thomas's justification of a righteous war (based upon St. Augustine's quotation from the words of John the Baptist to the soldiers!)* when such war is "waged by the command of the ruler, for a righteous cause and with a good intention," is in fact to assent to the inevitability of warfare and to exclude Christian pacifists from Churchmanship. Actually, as we all know, the general effect of the Catholic ethic is to foster the mediaeval eulogizing of militarism. Converts like Mr. Chesterton seem quite unable to realize that the age of the rapier and the blunderbuss has passed away and that modern conflicts are not waged after the pattern of the Napoleon of Notting Hill. And those like Mr. Orchard† who find their social and peace-loving convictions hard to reconcile with the inerrancy of Roman wisdom produce in their efforts to modify it an unedifying spectacle and much laborious but unconvincing special pleading. We have yet to learn that any loyal Roman Catholic could assent even to so temperate a pacifism as that of the last Lambeth Conference.

For in fact the standardizing of Christian obli-

* *Summa Theol.*, ii. 2, q. 40.
† Cf. his *From Faith to Faith*.

gation at a level which accommodates it to the demands of secular life has resulted in diminishing the influence of Christianity upon the development of human welfare and in exaggerating an otherworldly emphasis in the Catholic concept of saintliness. Few will deny that on the whole progress has been achieved in spite of rather than because of the Roman Church. Pioneers in every department both of knowledge and of social righteousness have almost invariably found the forces of Catholicism arrayed against them. It is not an accident that in the growth of enlightened citizenship one people after another has repudiated the papacy, and that none who have emancipated themselves show any signs of returning to allegiance. Democracy, as at present understood, may be open to the objections so freely brought against it in these difficult days: none of its champions is likely to be satisfied with the parodies of it under which we are now living. But the belief that it is the necessary corollary of the Christian ethic and that to abandon its pursuit would be not merely a tragedy but an apostasy is deep-seated. It haunts the generous mind, and challenges us to bring it down from heaven to earth. We shall not do so by reverting to mediaeval Catholicism, or by accepting the division of life into sacred and secular.

For along with the failure of Rome to come to terms with progress stands her commitment to a special type of saintliness—a type which many of us cannot accept as supreme. It has been well said that in all the long and varied list of the canonized only one name, St. Francis of Assisi, commands the full reverence of Christendom—and that because he is unique in his appreciation of the order of nature, and shared the characteristically Protestant delight in birds and flowers. It is, indeed, noteworthy and significant that the love of natural history* and concern for the study and welfare of animals is almost entirely lacking in Catholic countries. The cruelty to migratory birds in Italy and the brutality of Irish cattle-drovers are extreme cases of a general disregard. Saintliness, as usually and nowadays increasingly defined at Rome, lays stress upon supernatural virtues, by which is meant an absorbing other-worldliness, a cloistered and often ecstatic devotion. In many cases the canonized are demonstrably pathological, and though there are heroic exceptions the list contains few of the practical benefactors, the pioneers and emancipators of humanity.

VII

If the method of the double standard cannot be accepted, it remains for us to face the responsibilities of our freedom. This, and not the desire to temper the wind to the shorn lamb, is Christ's way. He does not legislate in detail, because He will not reduce discipleship to a slavish obedience. He will

* This is fully admitted and discussed from the Catholic standpoint in the very interesting preface by J. and J. Tharaud to J. Delamain's book *Why Birds Sing*.

not coerce or override; for He calls men His friends not His servants, and values voluntary loyalty so highly that He will accept the Cross rather than call for the legions of angels. He that has eyes to see, let him see: he that hath ears to hear, let him hear. There is the ethical principle of the Gospel.

So in the matter of war as in that of the ownership of wealth or slaves, Christ does not lay down particular rules universally applicable as tests of discipleship. He proclaims indeed a ministry of reconciliation which includes the love of enemies and the turning of the other cheek; and on occasion He bids His disciple put up the sword into its sheath, since to use it is to ensure destruction. So too He insists that man's life does not consist in the multitude of his possessions, utters awful warnings of the peril of riches and the folly of their pursuit, and bids the young ruler sell all that he has. It is plain enough that His revelation of God involves ultimately the reign of peace and the holding of all things in common. But men must learn the truth of this for themselves and accept it of their own free volition. He will not produce a programme which they can endorse mechanically or follow blindly. He will not bring in the kingdom by force or fiat. He sows a seed, a small thing but alive; a weak thing dependent for its growth upon the good partnership of soil and rain and sunlight, but capable of the miracle of organic increase; a living Word not a dead commandment, which He is content to entrust to the slow creative processes whereby His Father has achieved the evolution of mankind. We look back over the record of its development, and mark the awful vicissitudes to which it is exposed. The soil is obdurate—it is the soil of human hearts: the climate is fitful—drought and tempests succeed one another and restrict or distort the growing tree: often it seems stunted, often there is hardly a sign of leaf or blossom. Yet still it grows; and we begin to learn something of the heavenly gardener's care.

So surely it is in this matter of peace. Because the Church since its early days has not ventured to renounce war, that does not mean, any more than in the case of slavery, a permanent acquiescence in evil. Man is by heritage a pugnacious, as he is an acquisitive, animal. But, hard as it may be to sublimate his instincts, he is not condemned to a hopeless bondage to them. Slowly through the centuries, slowly and with many set-backs, certain evils are acknowledged and condemned. Always the Christian must be quick to recognize evil and resolute to challenge it. That we have failed before, that some of us are ready to fail again, is no excuse for those who have once seen the necessity for action.

In each generation, as it would appear, certain obvious opportunities are available for us. The obligation to full discipleship does not change: but in that fulness there are demands at present wholly beyond our range of consciousness. None of us can measure or appreciate what the coming of the Kingdom in every department of life would mean.

But we can see here and there definite steps to be taken. Then woe be to us if we fail. For when once we have accepted the challenge to mend our ways, a constraint is laid upon us; and to refuse is to sin unto death. If it be true that war is alien to the mind of Christ, then for His disciples there can be no further compromise. We may not judge others who have seen but not perceived: they were blind, and in our eyes also are beams. But we may not excuse ourselves by their example or be bound by their decisions. If now a vision of peace, not before granted, has been given, then at whatever cost we must be true to it.

CHAPTER V

THE CHRISTIAN AND THE USE OF FORCE

I

THERE will be no dispute that the known will of God can only be disregarded at the soul's peril. To see the good and to reject it is the sin of rebellion, the gravest of moral evils. But can we in the particular issue of war be thus certain?

We may indeed appeal with reasonable confidence to the teaching and life of Jesus. As we have seen, His educational method was by appeal to principle, not by explicit legislation. He sought to develop moral sensitiveness and to evoke intelligent co-operation, not to prescribe duties and compel obedience. But His principles are clear and He fulfilled them by the laying down of His life. The ethic of the Cross is love's plainest message, and it demonstrates that infinite suffering is to be preferred to coercion, that love endures all things rather than resort to violence. With this ethic His whole ministry is in accord. During the past twenty years the records have been sifted a thousand times in order to find justification for war. The arguments produced are so flimsy as to need no criticism. We are solemnly assured that the parable of the strong man armed—obviously Satan—proves the necessity of armaments; that the Apocalyptic discourse foresees the continuance of warfare—a pretext similar to the use of the words "The poor ye have always" to resist social legislation; and that the tragic exclamation "It is enough"—which comments upon the incorrigible blindness of the disciples—approves the taking of the two swords. In face of such perversities of exegesis comment is superfluous. Jesus is the Prince of Peace. That stands out from every witness to His work.

But, as we are rightly reminded, the example of Jesus must be studied against the background of God's other and continuous revelation. We have refused the antithesis between natural and revealed, and claim that in the study of the Universe, of the evolution and development of life and of humanity, is an unveiling of the character of God. I have argued at length elsewhere that the right procedure involves a bifocal vision of truth, that God can be and must be seen not only in Christ but in His world, that the whole range of our experience supplies necessary data for religion, and that the recent knowledge given us by the physical sciences must be taken into full account.

It is here that the most urgent difficulty in the advocacy of pacifism confronts us. If we are content to follow T. H. Huxley,* and to regard the moral conscience as protesting against and striving to reverse the movement of the natural order, our course is plain. We shall accept the evidence that

* Romanes Lecture on *Evolution and Ethics*.

nature is "red in tooth and claw" and ruled by the ethics of the jungle. We shall glorify Jesus just because in Him the revolt against nature reaches its climax. We shall accept a dualistic philosophy, and ascribe the ordering of evolution to the devil or the demiurge. As one of the most ancient and plausible solutions of the problem of evil, such a theory is entitled to respect; for though it is ultimately irreconcilable alike with Christianity and with theism it supplies a simple and often effective basis for moral effort.

For the Christian its failure is obvious. If God is responsible for the order of nature, then He must allow the existence of evil and of the devil and the problem remains unsolved. If He is not responsible and cannot overcome the devil, then He is not God. That Jesus accepted Him as Father and the Universe as within His purpose and control is manifest. The Church may have been wrong in silencing Gnostic argument by the appeal to tradition: it was certainly right in rejecting Gnosticism as a Christian philosophy. We are committed by every authority in Christendom to the belief in God as creator, not less than as redeemer and sanctifier, and in consequence to the belief that ultimately His activity as discernible in the Universe must display the same nature and purpose as His revelation in Christ. We must be prepared to check our conclusions in the one field by constant reference to the other, testing our gospel of love by the evidence of the evolutionary process, and our biology in the light of life's highest achievement, the manhood of Jesus.

Here for the pacifist arises his special difficulty.

II

No one who studies the record of living organisms can fail to recognize the formative influence of struggle upon their development. From amoeba to anthropoid the history of every species is the history of incessant and precarious war. By conflict against its fellows individual or type establishes its right to survive: by the destruction of other lives it maintains itself, by its own disappearance it pays the penalty for failure. With what ghoulish refinements of ingenuity survival value is achieved, with what horrors of greed and cruelty, of suffering and slaughter, progress is accompanied, every honest observer will admit. Those who find theism an easy faith or the doctrine of non-resistance an obvious ethic would do well to ponder upon the details of the struggle for existence. They will not be surprised that in the attempt to reconcile their belief in a moral purpose in nature with the facts of evolution the most sensitive minds of our generation are perplexed and aghast. There are times for most of us when the burden of it becomes almost intolerable, when we are tempted to curse God and die.

We must not shut our eyes to such facts, or protect ourselves against them by picking out the brighter side of the picture. It is indeed one of the dangers of the recent interest in nature that it tends to focus attention upon its beauty, upon the aesthetic appreciation of developing sensibilities, of mating and parenthood and co-operative effort, and to ignore the sterner, cruder aspects of the picture. Anthropomorphism colours our vision. Reaction against the Victorian stress upon carnage and elimination helps us to dismiss the evidence for them. Disgust at human error seeks a compensation in the faith that "all's well with the world" since "only man is vile." So we shirk the testing of our convictions and prefer an easy meliorism to the heartbreak of the effort to understand—as if religion were after all a search for comfort!

Yet when the element of struggle and its terrible consequences are fully recognized, I do not feel clear that Dr. Barnes* is justified in pronouncing ethical judgments upon the depravity of bacilli and parasites and in finding in them evidence of the non-moral character of evolution such as creates for us a new dilemma. For myself such evidence does not seem different from or so difficult as that which I know in my own character and see in the passion of Jesus. If we can accept His cry, "My God, my God, why hast thou forsaken me," at its full value, the existence of lesser tragedies does not seem to raise any fresh issue. The fact of sin (if sin is the right word to apply to the selfish will to live at levels below that of moral consciousness) is demonstrated in the crucifixion less crudely but

* In his Gifford Lectures, *Scientific Theory and Religion*, pp. 520-3.

surely far more poignantly than in the earlier struggles of the evolutionary process. If Judas and Caiaphas and Pilate, if my own cruelties and lusts, can be brought within belief in the love of God, it is not to me an additional problem to find the same kind of selfishness and ruthless disregard for others manifested at other stages of life's ascent. The Cross would lose something of its meaning if it were an isolated event, an unpredictable betrayal. If love's purpose involves the cost of Calvary, a similar price will surely be paid for every other step in the journey before and after. It has always been due, now in me, as of old at life's beginning. The currency may vary; the tribute take different forms: it remains a universal obligation.

We can, I suppose, accept the Cross of Christ because we see it not as the tragic failure of His earthly life but as a prelude to Easter, not as the triumph of wicked men but as the vindication of God's power to bring good out of evil. No doubt our knowledge of the sequel has in fact coloured our records of the calamity. Even in the Synoptists, and very clearly in the Fourth Gospel, the cry of dereliction is being modified and its bitterness explained away. The foreknowledge of Jesus is used to prevent the admission of a sense of defeat: He goes to His death not only willingly but (in St. John at least) as confident conqueror. His divinity, here as elsewhere, is supposed to release Him from the pain which others know—the pain of frustrated hope and despairing faith. Perhaps in so softening the tragedy we lose something of its meaning. Perhaps those who have insisted upon the loneliness and abandonment of His death have a lesson to teach us.

At least if we may look beyond the tragedy to its results in His case we must surely do so in our lesser Calvaries, even if in them the sequel is less immediate and dramatic. Whatever the details of evolution, the chief fact is that it moves, and moves onward and upward. It has produced mankind—that in our cynical moments may seem insufficient excuse: it has preluded the revelation in Christ. At each level, and as the consequence of the struggle, some new achievement has been gained, an achievement not merely in the range and complexity of the organism, but in the richness and the sensitiveness of its life. Always there is the incentive to adventure, the necessity for progress. The pressure of the environment, however much we may rebel against it, has been effective in producing out of the raw material of the living cell the agonies and ecstasies of the human spirit.

Truism as it is, such a result is too often forgotten. In the early days of the theory of evolution the necessary emphasis upon the struggle for existence and the survival of the fittest gave the impression that brute force, violence in attack and obduracy in defence, were the qualities fostered by the process. We fancied that the tiger and the elephant were its typical products and failed to realize that they were not in fact in the true line of succession and were already in danger of following the dragons and dinosaurs of the prime to extermination. In fact, of course, the development of immunity whether gained by tooth and claw or by easy diet and monstrous bulk is fatal to continuance. The race is not to the strong nor to the swift, but to the sensitive, the adaptable, I had almost said the suffering. Man's own descent is not from the lords of the jungle, but from creatures that have developed stereoscopic vision, the use of the hands, a highly organized vitality, a complex social life. And with the coming of man, though the end of the jungle is not yet, its day is over.

Is it too large a demand upon faith if we urge that when certain conditions are accompanied by certain definite developments we should assume a correspondence between them? We may not be able to prove that at each step cause and effect are exactly related: we certainly cannot explain the significance of every detail. A world without earthquakes or cancer, bacilli and parasites, blood and tears, is good to imagine and good to strive for. Dare we say that it could have produced the splendour of the Christ? Do we know enough to conclude that any single item in the overwhelming tale of suffering is unjustifiable? No one who reflects upon its course is likely to think of evolution with an easy optimism or to assume that all is for the best in this best of all possible worlds. We can perhaps only accept it when we have learnt to put a new meaning upon its worth and intention, to abandon our complacencies and our egoisms, and to realize that life on earth is always a journey and an adventure with a cross at the end of the road. Yet how few of us would deny that to be is better than not to be or, save for a moment, would welcome our own departure even into a dreamless sleep.

III

At this point it may be well to illustrate from experience the effects of an environment of danger and struggle upon the evolution of life. For by so doing we shall not only confirm the conclusions already reached, but disclose the next step in our argument—the answer to those who say that such struggle is essential to present progress and therefore that war is the great school of human virtue. It is from the war as I saw it in 1917 that my illustration is taken.

It was a curious coincidence that when I was suddenly accepted for service in France two subjects had long been specially perplexing me. One was the apocalyptic element in the Gospels, those strange predictions of calamity and judgment which seem to the sheltered scholar of to-day remote, fantastic, mistaken, and which some of us were busily trying to eliminate or to explain away. The other was this problem of evolution. To both my acquaintance with the front gave a vivid and unexpected illumination.

To go "up the line" was of course to enter an

apocalyptic world. All the material securities disappeared with the first screech of a shell. It was impossible to control events and useless to take thought for the morrow. War had already driven the more imaginative of our journalists to the language of the Book of Revelation: it showed me experiences which, if describable at all, demanded the imagery of darkened sun and falling heavens, of shattered earth and hearts fainting for fear. For civilized man to-day few things happen which he cannot foresee and provide for: he expects to go on with business as usual, to store up goods for many years and build barns for their reception: he is almost inevitably wrapped in the complacency of the rich fool. In the trenches this placid scheme was smashed beyond repair. Hell, the world of disorder, was let loose upon him. Monstrous happenings might befall him at any moment. In a day he might have to face without preparation emotional upheavals more intense, more varied, more continuous than he could experience in a life-time at home. Somehow he must find resources to meet them: somehow his organism must adjust itself to the strain. In such a life apocalyptic became sober truth—the only mode for depicting the life of the soul when it realizes the ardours and perils of its destiny.

It was in this discovery of the tension of warfare that light was thrown for me upon the process of evolution. In general that process is so slow that we can hardly see it at work even upon ourselves.

THE CHRISTIAN AND THE USE OF FORCE 135

We know, indeed, that certain changes in our environment occasionally take place: we can sometimes estimate their effects upon our characters. But to trace out the exact reaction of the self to circumstances, and to form any clear opinion of their formative influence, is difficult if not, normally, impossible.

In the war-zone evolution was "speeded up." The individual was hurled from one experience to another, to be shaped or broken, refined or distorted under their plastic surgery. In thirty-six hours in the battle of Cambrai I touched my life's extremes of anxiety and panic, of admiration and fellowship, of humour and horror. I have described elsewhere certain of the salient incidents: they are fairly typical of modern fighting and as such are worth reproducing here.*

"The thrills of a life-time were condensed into a day and forced upon one without disguise or preparation. All the conventional artifices by which civilized man shelters himself from the austerities and realities of elemental existence were stripped away. The real self stood naked to face the extremes of terror and of splendour. The impressions of those hours would take many pages to record: they surpassed my wildest dreams of hell and of heaven. Here are four out of very many.

"In a lull of the incessant barrage upon the sugar factory which was battalion headquarters I had to get from it to the aid post in the next building.

* *Musings and Memories*, p. 167.

Shelling was still intense: every inch of the ground was mangled and debris-strewn. Hurrying along over it I saw pinned beneath a tangle of broken beams and branches a soldier lying prone. He had the black grenade of my other battalion between his shoulders, and might be a friend. In any case, he might need help. I spent endless moments tearing away the litter, the enemy's guns hurrying my task: at length freed him; lifted his head;—and his face had been blown away.

"Twelve hours before I had been caught by shell-fire on a sunken-road—a howitzer–battery was traversing it up and down. In a scrape in the bank big enough to contain us I spent the next hour with an unknown private, huddled up and waiting for a direct hit. We could hear the gun fired, the flight of the missile, its scream and splash and roar, and the whizz of the pieces. Every half-minute a shell arrived, never more than a hundred yards away. The lad with me seemed unable to sit still: at last I warned him to stay quiet. A shell burst near: I saw his face: and realized that at each explosion he had put his body in the mouth of the hollow between it and me, offering his life for mine under conditions that try the manhood of the bravest.

"The aid post later that night, a cellar with six foot of wall above ground and constantly hit by direct fire: the bricks would withstand a light shell: a heavy or a 'dud' would have pierced them and brought the château down upon us. Within, a mass of casualties and assorted cases of shell-shock; a sergeant utterly unmanned, crying like a frightened child: a weedy youngster on a stretcher with three orderlies holding him down, and at every explosion a paroxysm in which he hurls the three about like a Samson. The doctor knew him: 'had shock before,' he murmurs to me: 'mother weak-minded: boy sent home once already: this will finish him for life.'

"A day later—the night after the grand attack. I go out through the wreckage to bury a pal shot the day before. Reaching the grave a shell bursts fifteen feet away, throwing me over, leaving me unwounded but unable to pronounce the letter S. Going back to the cellar two young officers who have got hold of a German machine-gun ask me to test its action. 'Come on, padre'—and I know that if I funk then, it will be all up with my manhood. Most unwillingly I go off with them, stuttering my readiness. We set up the gun: a shell explodes a few yards off and covers us with dirt. I find myself alone: the others are in retreat: I follow at speed. A moment's sheer panic—the real rabbit-in-a-trap spasm for perhaps five yards: then a roar of laughter as I race to shelter. Ten minutes later when my comrades reappear I present them with two noble pictures of our gun going into action and our gun-team in retreat. My lisp has entirely disappeared, and I sleep that night like a baby to find on waking that the colonel has wrapped me up in his own and only blanket.

"Horror and heroism, pathos and peril, fun and friendship—all the crucial events of life flung together with a speed that no artist dare attempt. Moments of excitement that reduce a football match to the *banalité* of a tea-party; moments of risk, with one's life as the stake; moments of waiting for the death that must surely come; moments of terror that make Grand Guignol tame: every fibre of one's being is tested, every chord in the range of one's soul is struck. Here are all the elements in man's career, all the elements in the struggle for existence, concentrated into a few days. Tell me of the liver-fluke or the praying mantis; I have seen cruelties more gruesome. Remind me of the glory of dawn in the mountains; I have known peaks of splendour more radiant and august. Nature in all its moods can be interpreted and surpassed in such experience."

Such incidents which fairly represent the range and *tempo* of life in battle put an almost unbearable strain upon the elasticity of one's power to respond to them. At first, like every other call upon vital resources, the effect is exhilarating and purgative. One becomes *exalté*, indifferent to the minor discomforts of existence, to fatigue and worry, thrilled with a tingling energy and the power to ride loose to life, cleansed as in great tragedy by the influence of pity and fear, intuitively sensitive to the claims and supports of comradeship. Here is an environment emotionally unlike that of civilized humanity, but recalling the grim intensity and crude simplicity of a primitive age.

Now the effect of this is equivalent to a speeding up of the evolutionary process, and of the development of character under its influence. Latent possibilities for good or evil, which might only have been disclosed by a decade of civil life and might then have been readily modified, sprang into full growth in a few hours. Unrecognized instincts, obscure streaks of vice or virtue, suddenly found expression. Men grew up in a week and were exhausted in a year. My own conviction is that most normal youngsters could stand the pace and even find excitement and inspiration for about six months: after that the strain began to disintegrate them; for the human organism is not geared up to such rapidity of change, and repeated shocks shake it to pieces: I do not think that anyone who had a consecutive year of actual front-line service has ever recovered from the effects of it—certainly not if he was in the infantry and in an active sector. That is, of course, why the United States never experienced the real stress of war at all: her army was only in the field long enough to see the best of it: it was spared the grim and inevitable tragedies of good men undermined, nerve slowly exhausted, character distorted and brutalized.

The stimulus of such accelerated reactions was at first and on the whole exhilarating. I should not claim that it was invariably ennobling. The speeding-up revealed ugly flaws of sensuality and cowardice, of cruelty and meanness. But on the whole men turned out vastly better than one expected. Nothing is more ignorant a libel than to denounce war as an orgy of lust and savagery: in fact there was an almost complete absence of sexuality in the trenches—the contrast between the line and the back areas in this respect was quite enormous—and a total disappearance of any personal hatred for the enemy. I lived for months in huts and dug-outs with men who certainly were not tongue-tied by respect for my cloth: I censored thousands of letters from a fighting battalion. Speech might consist of a monotonous repetition of two adjectives and two nouns, three of them originally obscene: but the atmosphere was cleaner and more humane than in most gatherings of men; and the delicacy of feeling, the respect for others, the generosity of outlook constantly filled me with wonder.

One becomes sensitive—that is the first lesson of it. Modern warfare, whatever may have been the character of earlier fighting, makes a larger demand upon the psychological than the physical resources. Most of the cases labelled shell-shock were caused not by some sudden explosion but by the failure of the organism to meet the demands upon it. For there comes a point at which sensibilities can respond no longer—a point of collapse.

Evolution fosters sensitiveness: that is a conclusion which I had not drawn from the story of the origin of species. I saw it clearly when I experienced its effects. It does so, not only because the emotional demands stimulate and enlarge one's range of reaction, but because it is the naturally sensitive that survive.

This second lesson of modern war is one which

many of those who only saw it at a distance fail to appreciate. For centuries we have assumed that military virtue was synonymous with muscular prowess, with solid, unimaginative, and rather animal temperaments. We expected the heroes of battle to be the heroes of the prize-fight or the football-field. Far be it from me to cast aspersions upon men of physical excellence and emotional placidity. But unless such qualities were accompanied by mental alertness, vivid imagination, and wide sympathies, their owners did not make good modern soldiers. The reason is obvious. Men whose physique set them above timidity and gave them a sense of superiority in school or college, now found fear, in a form in which their muscles availed nothing. Men who had never imagined horror were unmanned when they met it face to face. Men who had never wrestled with the riddles of life and reached some sort of conscious philosophy, now realized that the conventions and puerilities which had sufficed for peace-time crumbled away in the presence of death. In battle it was the bovine, not the highly strung, who succumbed to shell-shock: it was usually the sensitive, intelligent folk who displayed fantastic heroism and gained control of the situation and of their own fate. Homo sapiens, man with his full endowment of intellectual, psychic, and spiritual resources, made a better and a happier warrior than the tiger or the elephant. It is not an accident that evolution has given him the supremacy. The example of Rhys Davids, possibly the most valiant of all our heroes, indicates that it is in the class-rooms of Eton not upon its playing fields that the Waterloos of to-day are won; and Donald Hankey in his surprised eulogy of the Cockney soldier, precocious, imaginative, adaptable, but wholly lacking in all the traditional military virtues, in dignity, physical courage, and disregard of pain, pointed in the same direction.

IV

So far it may appear that in testifying to the influence of war to speed-up development and to foster sensitiveness I have been in fact justifying its value. In fact the significance of my illustration cannot be so interpreted.

In any case, of course, it does not pretend to disclose the full effects of war: the profiteers of Bradford and Dundee, the embusqués and the drawing-room soldiers of Whitehall, the propagandists of Parliament and Fleet Street, the pandars of the base-camps and back areas, the heroes of *Honours Easy*—all that sickening tale of war-victims would have to be added to the count; and in a sense they are a heavier indictment than the wreckage of homes, the mutilations and bereavements, the embitterment and dislocation of life; for those who exploit suffering are morally worse than those who are broken by it.

But confining ourselves to the fighting soldiery all that we have discovered is that up to a certain point the pressure of circumstances calls out the best in men, and that human nature under primitive conditions triumphs over the brute. We ought not to need the evidence of war in order to prove the worth of living dangerously. For the teaching of Jesus centres in the word "Whoso loveth his life loseth it; whoso loseth his life for my sake finds it"; and this is the secret of romance and the clue to the distinctively Christian ethic. The evil of war, even for those who get the best from it, lies in the fact that such tension even if endured and turned to gain is unnatural in itself and unworthy in its objective—unnatural because it is a reversion to an environment that we have long outgrown, unworthy because the purpose of our agony is ultimately the crude intent to kill.

Mankind is no longer organized for conflict at this level. He has grown out of the age of the cave-dwellers, and though his civilization has not destroyed but enhanced his powers of resistance, the breaking-point is speedily reached. To me, I confess, the saddest experience of war was not death or even maiming: it was the spectacle of lads who had revealed splendid qualities of fortitude and comradeship being demoralized by the continuance of the test. Sherriff in *Journey's End* has given us a picture that most of us could multiply a hundred-fold. Sooner or later the character can no longer endure: its vitality is exhausted, its elasticity outworn. Stimulants may have their value: to live on them is to become a wreck; and such wreckage of the best was pitiable to see. When we complain of the dearth of leaders in these post-war years, we think chiefly of the casualty lists: we forget that every man who was not fortunate enough to get out of the line by promotion or wound, and who saw more than a year's fighting, has sacrificed his future. We cannot wonder that since the war the prizes of prestige and position in Church and State have gone almost exclusively to the men who stayed at home. They have preserved a fitness which others lost under the tension of reiterated shocks.

Such endurance, so splendid and so tragic, might be justified if the end were divine. The man who will not fling his life away for a cause is not fit for earth or heaven. But it is folly and wastage, idolatry and sacrilege, to demand such an offering for any but the highest service. Man, civilized and Christian, should have outgrown the stage at which he can worship Caesar, or deify the Empire, or give his life to political and economic aggrandizement. No doubt it is better to seek his nation's victory than his own comfort or wealth: no doubt men still surrender to baser ends than warfare: no doubt every sacrifice to public opinion or to tribal god brings a measure of reward. But the best should be given only to the highest. God alone deserves and should receive the testimony of martyrdom. If the glamour of the cause in 1914 seemed to many of us divine, if patriotism seemed a sufficient altar for the supreme sacrifice, these bitter decades have surely convinced us of our error. It is, after all,

THE CHRISTIAN AND THE USE OF FORCE

nearly two thousand years since a great warrior of the Spirit bade us be "no longer children tossed to and fro and carried about with every wind of doctrine, by the sleight of men and cunning craftiness whereby they lie in wait to deceive." Are those last words too strong a description of the public opinion, of the hysteria and the propaganda, to which we succumbed? Warfare was a relapse into the childhood of the race.

Here in the matter of evolution, as previously in the matter of Christian history, it is not my intention to deny the value of certain methods in the past, but only to insist that they belong to the past not to the present. The world is so ordered that at every level "life and life more abundant" can only be won by effort: to relax the effort is to die. At first that effort is largely devoted to physical struggle: the organism is equipped for nothing else. But as in the lapse of time more complex creatures are evolved, other elements enter in. Consciousness becomes purposive, interests more varied; the will to live is no longer satisfied with bodily sustenance and preservation. In the conflicts of the higher animals psychic factors enter and gain increasing importance;* and the object of struggle is no longer only to kill or to avoid being killed. Life gains a new richness as new capacities emerge; and the struggle, as there is much evidence to prove, becomes less crude and wanton. There are few pictures of nature

* See the mass of evidence for "psychological warfare" in Hingston, *Animal Colour and Adornment*.

so false as those which represent the structure of birds and mammals as determined solely by its utilitarian value and their lives as overshadowed by the constant endeavour to slay or to escape. Other instincts than that of self-protection are at work; other elements than the presence of the enemy enter increasingly into their range of interest.

With man and the emergence of new levels of psychic and spiritual achievement the transformation of the struggle for existence proceeds more rapidly. If physical force still enters in and in early times counts for much, its importance steadily diminishes, as man's satisfactions cease to be centred in his body. Fretted as he is by his inheritance of animal instincts and by the antagonism of flesh and spirit man can no longer regard his bodily welfare as an end in itself. He is no longer content with the preservation of life unless life can serve some purpose which he accepts as good. He is restless and unhappy until he can find some prospect of integrating the conflicting elements in his nature, of "preserving body, soul, and spirit entire." How to achieve unity of personality in a world of claims and counterclaims becomes more and more his conscious quest.

Three possibilities confront him. He can capitulate to the flesh: but this is to relapse into animalism. There is no satisfaction there; for the distinctively human elements in his nature cannot be eradicated or permanently denied. He can draw a hard line between physical and spiritual, formulate a dualistic philosophy, and seek mortification of the one element and illumination of the other. The great religions of the East, whether they represent the physical as positively existent and actively diabolical, or deny its reality and describe its experiences as illusion, have followed this road. They aim at the emancipation of spirit from matter, rather than at the sublimation of matter to the harmonious service of spirit. The third course accepts the value of the physical, but insists that such value can only be fulfilled if the body is redeemed and brought under the control of the spirit. The body has its legitimate needs and uses: its activities are not necessarily evil. But these can only be satisfied as they conform to the requirements of the whole nature and as these are dictated by the aspirations of the man's best self. Such a position includes a full recognition of the physical and a measure of renunciation in bringing it into subjection. But its outlook is radically different from dualism, and its method is that of transformation, not of suppression. Christianity, though it has at times been powerfully influenced by Gnostic illuminationism and by Manichean asceticism, is committed by its doctrines of Incarnation and Atonement to a redemptive and sacramental philosophy.

With the theory of evolution Christians, despite the lamentable controversies of the last century, have no grounds for quarrel. Indeed, the first theology of the Church, the Logos-doctrine of the early Greek Fathers, was wholly evolutionary. They saw the process of history as one of the continuous training of mankind by the educative Word. Heraclitus and Socrates, Moses and the Prophets were ministers of the Christ, and tutors under His guidance of mankind. Step by step man was being helped to grow up out of the crude animalism of his infancy into the ordered freedom of maturity, and so onward to the measure of the fulness of the stature of Christ. They saw that the task was long: they recognized the obstinacy of old habits, the evidence of frustration and reversion. They claimed that in Jesus the final stage of the journey had been begun, its goal displayed, its inspiration given. Logos, by which they meant not merely the mind but the spirit, was king, and sooner or later His sovereignty would be acknowledged. Meanwhile, progress in the task of disciplining the lower impulses must be continued, and the Church must see that there was no turning back to earlier stages of the way and no slackening in the search for perfection. War to them was a reversion and a betrayal of the faith. Its place was taken by the spiritual conflict to which the race was now commissioned.

This last point is important. We have seen that the fact of struggle appears to be an essential formative condition of development, that it is only in the ceaseless effort for fulness of life that life can be maintained. Yet with the emergence of new levels of experience the character of the struggle changes. To devote to physical effort, to expose to physical tension, capacities adapted to higher use, is to prostitute them—it is to misuse the body and to outrage the spirit.

That is the evolutionary case against war—that it subjects a highly organized creature to conditions which, if they ever had a eugenic justification, have now become not creative but disintegrating. It is nonsense to say that civilization has enervated the race, or that war is necessary to prevent man from becoming soft and degenerate. No one who compares the recent war with its predecessors will regard human valour as diminishing or human endurance as undermined by increasing culture. The demands upon fortitude in a single day of modern battle were greater than in a life-time of previous campaigning. Humanity has never been exposed to an ordeal so fierce as the battle of the Somme or Passchendaele or the retreat to Amiens. And the most civilized stood the test most successfully. But in doing so they were squandering capacities adapted for high cultural and religious ends upon crude and barbarous efforts. To devote the finest susceptibilities of mankind to the business of escaping and inflicting physical torture is to use a surgeon's scalpel to do the work of a frontiersman's axe. We have no right to forfeit the hard-won gains of the ages and to revert to primitive methods for conducting modern life. Those who reflect upon the characters of men like Leslie Johnston or Charles Sorley, of Tom Allen or Arthur Adam will realize the iniquity of such waste.

Stated simply, our contention is this. The task of

evolution, which is surely the purpose of God, is not to eradicate the tigerish and ape-like elements in human nature, but to sublimate and transform them. Faculties originally developed in conditions of physical conflict have now become fit for altruism and for religion. Warfare sets back the clock and thereby sins against the whole significance of life. It may vindicate the value of sensitiveness: it misuses, blunts, and eventually smashes the finest instrument of progress, the noblest product of the travail of the ages. Man has struggled through history to reach integration of character and a world-wide co-operative society. Just when the goal is clearly seen and an effort to attain it is practicable, we are flung back into an orgy of mutual suicide. The tiger and the ape break loose, and as subsequent events have shown all prospect of progress is thwarted until they can be brought back into the submission which is their true end.

V

It will be seen that the position here reached, though in its main conclusion similar to that of other pacifists, is not based upon nor consistent with any wholesale objection to the use of physical force. As sometimes stated, the denunciation of physical force seems to me to involve a contempt for the body which is almost Manichean, and to be certainly inconsistent with a truly incarnational philosophy. Our business is to consecrate the flesh, not to eliminate it, to make it the instrument of the spirit not to despise it as a source of contamination. I do not believe that wedded love which denies itself physical expression is necessarily higher or purer thereby. Nor, if love can ever punish, am I convinced that bodily chastisement is always to be condemned. The defence of peace is no doubt easier if one can draw a hard line: but here as elsewhere the argument when so drastically simplified seems to become neither theoretically sound nor practically demonstrable.

This does not, of course, imply that the end always justifies the means, that, for example, in education any method effective in securing the teacher's objective is therefore justifiable, or that it is legitimate to work for human brotherhood by the bombs and bayonets of red revolution. It does definitely mean that I cannot say as some would do that Christ could not possibly have used a scourge of small cords; that in the training of children there may be occasions on which a smacking is the best possible treatment; and that among adults I can conceive of circumstances under which physical force is legitimate and necessary. Such an admission involves consequences which cannot honestly be avoided and which for me constitute the crux of the whole problem.

If physical struggle has played a beneficent part in evolution, and if in the training of the young there is still a stage at which physical force is the appropriate argument, then the question of warfare among backward peoples becomes at once open. Many of us who would assert without hesitation that war between Christian and cultured men is as out-of-date as duelling cannot so promptly denounce it when used against those to whom it seems the only effective instrument. It is the situation in Palestine or on the North-West frontier that is the serious obstacle to a policy of total and immediate disarmament. For here we are dealing with peoples whose whole training, tradition, and religion glorifies the warrior, whose power to kill is at present restrained by the use of superior military force, and from whom we are pledged to defend men and women who would otherwise be their victims.

The difficulty is not eased if it be urged that we have no business to be in India, and that the Zionist policy was a mistake. The "white man's burden" is no doubt a pretext that has been used to excuse much greed and some arrogance. Our motives, like those of other human beings, have been and are sadly mixed. But if it was wrong to undertake such obligations, the fact remains that they are fastened upon us, and that to repudiate them is not necessarily either expedient or morally defensible. For under the pledge of security offered by our occupation, great civilizing activities are being carried on; and peaceful multitudes are living in reliance upon our protection. Any one of us is entitled and may be bound to accept martyrdom for ourselves: to expose to it innocent folks who have settled in countries kept secure by our garrisons is a quite different moral issue. So long as Islam encourages its followers to death in battle against the infidel as the surest road to heaven, and as Afghan and Arab tribesman live in hope of a day of ravage and massacre, it is not easy to vote for the withdrawal of the legions. In dealing with those to whom force is the only restraint are we not spiritually bound to use the effective means?

Nor does it seem morally right to vote for a policy of disarmament if one is not convinced that it is immediately practicable. It may be that the majority will certainly refuse to evacuate Palestine or to disband the regiments on the frontier, and that therefore the citizen who adopts uncompromising pacifism can do so without running any risk of seeing his programme put into effect. But to vote for it on that assumption is surely a questionable use of citizenship. It is difficult to get rid of the conviction that there is something morally wrong in voting for a policy if, supposing one were a dictator, one could not put it into immediate effect. Would those who so earnestly support full disarmament take the responsibility for acting upon their convictions? If not, are they not in the position of crying for the moon, in the hope that thereby they may at least stimulate their fellows to move up a story nearer to the roof of the house? Possibly such a method is effective; but it surely causes very many to dismiss their plea as Utopian and themselves as moonstruck. Unless an immediately available alternative to the method of military constraint can be found, the extreme pacifist position is not, I fear, likely to commend itself to practical citizens.

This has been to me for some years a serious obstacle. To cry for no more war and to sign petitions in favour of total disarmament or pledges to abstain from any sort of military action is a delightfully simple course. Its value admittedly arises from the fact that a Government, if aware that a sufficient number of its nationals would under all circumstances refuse to fight, would have to take the demand for peace seriously and could not wantonly plunge its people into warfare. We may, perhaps, dismiss the argument that such pledges merely encourage military powers to stir up war against us by answering that this implies the old and rotten belief that to prepare for war is the best preservative of peace. But if it is true that in certain areas of the globe military action is still the only alternative to wholesale massacre, to say "you may defend them; I will not" is an attitude hard to accept; and if it is not true, then surely our business is not merely to abstain from one course of restrictive action but to advocate and to undertake another.

Is war the only appropriate instrument? Is there any other way open to us? That question is obviously urgent.

CHAPTER VI

THE CHRISTIAN AND THE ALTERNATIVE TO WAR

I

OUR contention hitherto has been that in the course of evolution the struggle for existence has become increasingly an effort to achieve moral and spiritual values; that in history we can see the gradual development of man's appreciation of such values; that this development takes place step by step as accepted standards are challenged and primitive instincts sublimated, and that in this matter of war we have now reached a point at which it has become an intolerable anachronism. Yet if we are to outgrow it there is need both to provide an alternative method for effecting the purposes now served by military activity (so far as those purposes are ethically desirable) and to convince the race that in this alternative is to be found a fuller satisfaction than war could give. Man will not abandon war so long as he thinks it the only means for saving himself from destruction; he will not be educated out of it unless he can find other fields for the exercise of the qualities hitherto associated with battle. If there is a more excellent way promising better results and demanding a higher type of sacrifice, then to persist in war should become unthinkable.

That there is a more excellent way is surely axiomatic for the Christian. Whatever his views as to the legitimacy of physical force or as to the case for war, he must admit that if justifiable at all it is only so as a last resort and as a second best. Even the most ardent militarist would only allow an appeal to arms when other methods were of no avail: if he were a Christian he would have to go further and allow it only if love made it necessary to strike.

Here is a paradox which to some will seem at once an absurdity. We are told to love our enemies and do them good. It may be arguable that the best thing we can do to them is to punish them, and that physical punishment is the only appropriate remedy. I should not myself rule out such an argument; for I have admitted that there may be individuals and occasions that demand the loving use of force. But as has often been urged we do not in these days adopt the method of the "whipping-boy": if certain people have raided our territory and killed our folk, to send aeroplanes and bomb their homes is to use a type of reprisal which in civil life we have long ago abandoned. "I can't catch the murderer; but I'll torture his wife and kill his baby: that will show him that he must mend his ways" might be effective: it could hardly be regarded as just or as humane. If we shelter ourselves behind the doctrine of collective responsibility in the one case, why not in the other?

Love may perhaps smite. Is it ever justified in

killing—in following Caiaphas's principle that it is expedient for one man to die for the people? Many of us are coming to feel that even in the case of the worst of crimes, capital punishment is neither justifiable nor, indeed, effective. Yet it is surely far easier to defend the right of a community to demand the death penalty for murder than to vindicate the wholesale slaughter of modern warfare. It must be a desperate case which leaves us with no other remedy. We could surely only accept so hideous a "second best" if it were demonstrable that every other possibility had been tried and found futile. Will anyone be bold enough to urge that this has, in fact, in any single case been done?

It is here, surely, that the analogy between the use of the police in the treatment of crime and of soldiery in war—an analogy of very doubtful worth, but much employed by the critics of pacifism—gives us a result very different from what is usually put forward. We are always being asked whether, if we refuse to countenance military action, we would allow lunatics or burglars to terrorize or hold to ransom the community. For myself, as has been already indicated, the answer to such a question would be that in fact the cases are not identical. We may not yet have reached the level at which coercive restraint of moral imbeciles and criminals can be superseded, though even here on sound principles we refuse to arm the police with revolvers, and regard their task as reformative not retributive. War is a different matter; it is indiscriminating in its effects, retributive in its intention, and unsatisfactory in its results. Moreover, whereas every educational and social effort is used to discourage crime, no such effort has been used in those types of warfare as, for example, against frontier tribesmen where the parallel is least inappropriate. In the one case force is only used when other methods have been tried; in the other it is the first and almost the sole remedy to be employed.

No doubt there can be quoted instances both of police action and of war in which the line between them is hard to draw. It may even be probable that the next step in getting rid of warfare will be the restriction of armies to the duties for which civil guards exist. But in any case the Christian, if he is true to the principles of his Master, is surely bound to maintain that any philosophy or policy which assumes that force and not love is the ultimate sanction and basis of government is to be condemned; that punishment must aim at the reform of the offender not at vengeance upon him; and that alike in domestic and in international affairs the facts of evolution not less than the teaching of Christ demand the replacement of physical by spiritual agencies. If so, then the Christian must challenge every use of force with the question "Is this love's best way?" So challenged, it is to me at least clear that war can be isolated from all other lines of action and condemned as violating the fundamental principles of Christ's religion.

II

For the Christian the suggestion that killing is the appropriate argument should arouse an immediate repudiation. If God is the Father, if creative love is the source and stay of our being, then can we under any circumstances admit that the best that we can do for a person is to put an end to his life? It seems to me that it is far easier to justify an overdose of morphia in a case of incurable and agonizing disease than to put to death a possibly reformable criminal, and that neither of these provides any excuse for war. There are no doubt men and tribes who still think fighting a splendid and holy thing. We are ourselves only beginning to grow out of that belief. It was universal in the time of Christ. Yet He did not accept it, or allow it to lead Him to meet swords with swords. It was plain to Him, it was plain even to His disciples, that His enemies sought to kill Him. Humanly speaking, flight or resistance—that is the admission that the issue depended in the last resort upon military power—was the only practicable course. He refused to take it and forbade it to His followers. He saw it as the way of destruction—"they that take the sword perish by the sword"—a destruction without redemptive value. Rather let the warriors do their worst. The Cross should be His answer. He had used every other instrument in the armoury of love, had used it to the uttermost, and without avail. One only remained. His last appeal was not the warrior's but the martyr's. Love won by the arbitrament not of struggle but of suffering.

Martyrdom is the Christian's ultimate obligation—to lay down his life for his friends. Even in these days of conventional religion when the demands of Christ have been cheapened and made trivial there have been many who have spared not their lives. If we are to get rid of war, it may be that the old obligation will have to be accepted afresh. But, for our present argument, the alternative to war is not necessarily so drastic. We have not yet exhausted, we have indeed hardly set ourselves to try, other ways.

Here is the tragedy of it. In theory all Christians would admit that human nature is capable of responding to Christ—that to obey His appeal is God's will for us, and that God's will is mankind's true welfare. In such a faith we evangelize and educate, believing that the good news is appropriate as much to the black and brown and yellow races as to the white, that in them all is the capacity to respond to it, that for them all Christianity is the only and a practicable religion. Yet in our politics we dismiss this conviction as fantastic. Conquest must be by military action—order must rely upon bayonets: the big battalions speak the first and last word. When the armed forces of the Crown have established the *pax Britannica*, then the civilizing agencies can get to work. But the first line of defence is a line of forts not of schools. Missionaries are beginning to realize that this is hardly a gracious method of commending their message, that indeed it raises doubts as to the sincerity of Christian Britain. But reliance upon it among statesmen is still axiomatic. It has been left to Mahatma Gandhi to challenge the assumptions on which it is based, and to raise doubts as to whether the weak things of this world are not even to-day stronger than the strong.

Yet surely the experience of the past century might encourage us to put our faith a little more vigorously into practice. Take the case of Central Africa as an example. It was by missionaries that the land was explored and opened up; and if, as in Uganda, their first efforts led to outbreaks of persecution, the martyrs did not die in vain. For a time it was the facile comment upon them that they destroyed the native virtues and appealed only to the weaklings. Then it was argued that in the race for the soul of the African Islam was bound to win; for it recognized warfare and polygamy and was adapted to the moral standards of the tribes. Now when Christian communities are securely established, and when the character of the converts and the influence of Christ upon the tribal life can no longer be questioned, we are beginning to realize that the religious, educational, and medical services, far more than the military, are responsible for the peace of the land. It is highly significant that in areas like the Gold Coast where our administration has been most enlightened it has also been most successful; and that in them a stress is laid upon the value of religion and of religious education greater than is the case even in Europe. As a peacemaking agency the gospel of Christ has proved its power.

This is surely a point worth emphasizing; for the experience of the past century in evangelism is an important factor in supporting the claims of Christianity. So long as the Church was mainly confined to Europe or as its missionary work merely followed the flag, it might be argued that the "backward races" could only be dealt with by force: conquer first and convert, if you can, afterwards. The example of the early Quakers in America and of certain heroic Roman Catholics could indeed be urged against it. But on the whole it went unchallenged. Now in every continent missionaries have shown the possibility and the power of the unarmed approach. Taking their lives in their hands they have adventured among peoples traditionally warlike, among cannibals and primitive tribes, in regions hitherto unvisited. The record of their courage and perseverance, of their labours in learning, reducing to writing, and translating the Scriptures into unknown tongues, and in introducing medical, agricultural, and civilizing benefits, of their success in breaking the power of ancient fears and taboos, in reconciling feuds and putting a stop to bloodshed, are among the most romantic stories in human history. They have triumphed over every sort of opposition abroad and of ill-report at home: they have vindicated the uniqueness and the universality

THE CHRISTIAN ALTERNATIVE TO WAR

of the Christ: they have laid the foundations of a world-wide Christian commonwealth. In no period of its history has the Church seen so clear a proof of its divine resources.

Encouraged by such evidence Christians have, now less than ever, no excuse for accepting the conventional belief in the arm of the flesh. Easy talk, "war is the religion of the Arab," "the only argument for an Afridi is a bullet," if it was ever true, need be accepted as such no longer. For we have now a plain and proven alternative; and can point to multitudes of examples in which it has been effectively used. There are still places and peoples to which we have hardly begun to apply it: that is true. To do so would involve danger and might well cost precious lives: that is also true. But neither argument should persuade us that war is the only way; indeed, each should stimulate us to greater and more immediate effort.

III

It is in the service of Christ's religion that a moral equivalent and a suitable substitute for warfare can be found. Instead of assuming that life can only be secured by garrisons the Christian should insist that love is stronger than fear; that no peace based upon coercion can ever be stable; and that the power of the Gospel has been sufficiently demonstrated to be worthy of a trial even from the standpoint of the statesman. A negative pacifism, a mere refusal to fight, is open to grave criticism: a positive effort to establish the sovereignty of the Prince of Peace is of the essence of Christian discipleship. Surely the one involves the other. Surely in these days it is full time that we realized the new possibilities of world-wide comity opening before us: realized that warfare was fatal to their fulfilment: realized that to achieve them would demand a wholehearted sacrifice, a fortitude and a zeal, not less exacting though infinitely more satisfying than those required of the soldier. To the wider possibilities of the time we will refer later. First the claim of Christianity to sublimate the instincts hitherto devoted to battle must be considered.

To do so is to insist upon a concept of Christianity still not too common. We have for so long regarded religion as a comfortable refuge in this life and a useful insurance for the life to come that its austerities and romance have been almost forgotten. There has been of late an attempt to strip some of the more obvious sentimentalities from the Christian concept of love; to counteract the one-sided emphasis upon the gentleness of Jesus; to reveal the passion and heroism of the Son of God alongside of His mercy and suffering. Criticism has helped us to dethrone the mild preacher of social righteousness by its recent recovery of the apocalyptic and austere elements in His teaching. It has warned us against applying word for word the injunctions given by His apostles to their converts in days when the Churches were little groups of helpless folk for whom quietness and passivity were the only practicable methods. It has shown us the revolutionary character of the changes that Christianity demanded and the indomitable courage and resourcefulness of its leaders, as we have come to study them not as figures in stained glass, but as living, striving, suffering men. But though there has been a change, it is still far from complete. The Bible is still regarded not as the reformer's hand-book, but as what Kingsley called it, "an opiate dose for keeping beasts of burden patient while they were being overloaded."* The Church still seems synonymous with Pleasant Sunday Afternoons or mysterious creeds and sacraments, and concerned rather with escape from the world than with its redemption. The Ministry is still "not quite a man's life," a soft and respectable rather than an exacting and dangerous profession. And while this is the public estimate, it will appear to many merely ridiculous to suggest that in the religion of Christ the warrior can find unique opportunity for the employment and satisfaction of his highest virtues. Yet that, I believe, is quite literally the fact.

Of course it must be confessed that Christians have only themselves to blame if they are regarded as weak and ineffective. Humility is the strongest thing in the world: we have often made it appear the most timid. Purity is an austere and positive idealism: we have degraded it into an anaemic and savourless abstinence. Compassion is an agony of

* In *Politics for the People*, p. 58.

faith and pain, not a complacent benevolence or a hearty and easy-going optimism. Worship is not an ecstasy of escape from the real world, but an inspiration to give one's life in its service. To set down such contrasts is to be reminded how fatally our practice contradicts our profession.

Moreover, if the Church has been content to follow the flag, allowing military and commercial interests to be the pioneers and then striving when they have established themselves to mitigate some of the effects of their supremacy, the same procedure has too frequently happened in other fields. Christ was a pioneer. In the early years His followers were not afraid to criticize and break away from the established usages of society and to strike out new lines of thought and conduct. To-day we find it easy to condemn the compromise with the world that is symbolized by the conversion of Constantine. We feel that when the Church came to terms with the Empire and accepted the rightfulness of its military, civic, and social system, something not far from a betrayal of religion was involved. But we do not seem to recognize how deeply our own attitude is still tainted with similar compromise. If we condemn the Christian acquiescence in war, is it not reasonably certain that a century hence our Christian successors will equally condemn us for accepting without serious demur an industrial system of which the stock market, the advertising agency, and what Carlyle called the cash-nexus are essential parts and in which acquisitiveness and competition are the master motives? The record of the Church's hostility to the scientific movement in the last century or to the social experiments of to-day is hardly conspicuous for its adventurousness. We allow the secular arm to blaze the trail, occasionally begging it not to forget the claims of religion, more often denouncing it for threatening to disturb our vested interests. Then when it has added new provinces to man's dominion we rather timidly enter into them and see how far they can be brought to acknowledge Christianity. If we really want a moral equivalent for war, we have only to set ourselves to remove its economic causes or to take seriously our Master's teaching about money. Some of our Communist contemporaries could tell us how fierce a struggle would be the consequence.

Of course it is not intended to suggest that there are no Christians who live out their discipleship in a spirit of adventure and of uncompromising devotion. In spite of what has been said, it would be easy to compile a list of Christian pioneers, and to show that, in addition, it is among the members of the Churches that movements for reform find their strongest support. But our concern is not only to prove that rightly understood and faithfully followed Christianity involves a life of more than military self-surrender, but to claim that in it the ordinary man here and now can find a moral equivalent to war. This latter will hardly be admitted so long as the mass of Christians fails to realize and to live up to its vocation; and few of us dare assert that this is not the case. Most of us have either made ourselves at home in the world, and despite occasional stings of conscience are successfully comfortable and respectable, or we have fled from it, persuading ourselves that the really important thing in religion is not world redemption or world evangelism, but the punctilious performance of the duties of the sanctuary and the cultivation of private and often esoteric virtues.

Herein of course is an illustration of the old adage *corruptio optimi pessima*, of the principle that to fail of the best is usually to attain not the next best but the very opposite of what we sought. It is abundantly plain to anyone who has seized the meaning of apocalyptic and of its place in the thought of Jesus that His desire was to awaken men to vision, to startle or charm them into life. He seems to have felt not that we were rebels and sinners so much as blind and dull and insensitive, concealing our lack of vitality by much praise of caution and thrift and prudence. He preferred (dare we say it?) a spendthrift vice, the harlot whose sins were forgiven because she loved much, to a niggardly and calculating virtue; a romantic and impulsive recklessness to anxiety and introspection; a vivid and intuitive imagination to the learning of the schools. To ride loose to life, counting it well spent if lost for loyalty; to live from hour to hour, savouring to the full its joys and pains; to be swift to catch the significance of the moment, and to turn it to good account; above all to centre one's interest

THE CHRISTIAN ALTERNATIVE TO WAR

upon persons not upon things; such was the way of living which He revealed and strove to create. Some of us found our clearest experience of it when we had come to terms with death and found ourselves freed from fear and pride in the comradeship of shared suffering. We knew it for the first time in the trenches, and realized that it was theoretically familiar: we had already found it and failed to recognize it in the Gospels.

We have urged that though for many of us war was our first introduction to romance (if that is the right word for Christ's characteristic ethic), this does not justify war or imply more than that we had never understood our religion. In fact, of course, romance can be discovered without any necessity for physical strife. For its full realization there are, as it seems, three necessary conditions—conditions by no means limited to battle.

The first is the possession of a satisfying ideal, an ideal which can call out a passionate devotion and draw all our energies to its attainment. Ideal is too cold and abstract a term. Human beings demand that it be embodied for them in a person. Only when a man or nation sees its dream incarnate is its transformation complete. For, if it is to integrate and sublimate, devotion must quicken into love; that is why the art of loving is the highest and hardest part of education: and love, as Dr. Lloyd Morgan would argue,* cannot be given except poetically, metaphorically

* *Life, Mind and Spirit*, p. 275.

and improperly to the inanimate or the sub-human.

The second is the possession along with the ideal of some great and concrete task to be performed for its sake. Vision, unless it is expressed in action, enervates: love, unless it gives itself in service, turns rotten. To arouse enthusiasm and to deny it an outlet is to leave the enthusiast frustrate and resentful: his second state is worse than his first: it were well for him if his passion had never been born. The task must be worthy of the love, a task impossible (humanly speaking) of fulfilment, a task calling out all the resources of courage and patience, of ingenuity and persistence. It is in the doing of the work that the quality of the ideal is disclosed and its power to inspire appropriated.

The third is the support and inspiration of fellowship. Just as, in the individual, integration of character puts an end to inward conflict and releases for higher use the energies wasted upon it, so, as we discover friendship and can cease to arm ourselves against our neighbours, a flood of new vitality becomes available. It is a commonplace that the valour of comrades differs vastly from the sum of their individual courage; and the same is true of any real group activity. We are used to the idea that the crowd or the committee almost invariably falls below the level of its more enlightened members. Collective action of a higher type, where the agents can be described as "of one mind and of one soul," has exactly the opposite effect: it transcends the uttermost that its members could separately accomplish; and they find themselves sustained and impelled by its influence.*

The classic example of the fulfilment of these three conditions is to be studied in the earliest Church. The disciples had learned loyalty, losing their self-esteem in the shame of their betrayal and assured of their Master's triumph by His resurrection. He had commissioned them to a superhuman adventure, the evangelizing of the world; and the greater the demand the more certain the response. In shared devotion and shared service they had been welded into a community of the Spirit, becoming literally incorporated into a single and emergent organism, the Church or body of Christ. As such they found a way of life more exacting, more rewarding than military service in the warfare against principalities and powers and the enthroned evil of the world.

IV

"May God deny thee peace and grant thee glory"; so Unamuno finishes his poignant and profoundly moving book. Peace can so easily become a synonym for ease and prosperity that unless we can present its claims in terms of romance and adventure, men at their best will surely spurn it. We have urged from the first that the appeal to dread and disgust

---

* This is of course the answer to Niebuhr's contention that society or men acting corporately are necessarily immoral.

or to security and material advantage does disservice to the cause; and it is perhaps on this account that so many Christians have seemed backward in its advocacy.

If we would work for peace there is indeed urgent need for denunciation of war, for insistence upon its outlawry and upon consequent disarmament, for watchful efforts to forestall occasions of dispute and for the removal of the economic evils that are its cause. Such work need not be negative or palliative. At its best it is inspired by a passionate desire to lift the cloud which now threatens to overwhelm our civilization, and to set human energies free for nobler and more constructive aims. But for the Christian it may well be true that his immediate business is rather to throw himself heart and soul into the more direct service of world evangelism. For he will feel that the only radical cure for war is the freeing of mankind from pride and aggression, the revealing to them of the worth and demands of the life of the Spirit and the fashioning of them into a sensitive and generous fellowship.

It is surely unnecessary to argue that in these days the old theory of the self-sufficient, self-contained nation has become untenable; that international co-operation and acceptance of a supernational allegiance are essential to human welfare; that the basis for such unity cannot be found unless there is a measure of agreement as to the values of life and the principles of conduct; and that the most universal and powerful human motive, the influence of religion, is alone capable of creating and sustaining such unity.

In view of the present outbreak of national and racial feeling, not only in Asia and Africa but among European peoples who might be expected to have learnt the lesson of 1914, even the first of these very obvious convictions may nowadays be temporarily challenged. That a war so long and so embittered would accentuate old animosities was inevitable. The Treaty of Versailles did little to allay and much to intensify them. The economic pressure inflicted a period of cruel hardship upon Germany and especially upon the educated classes, and the procrastination of the victors in proceeding to the disarmament foreshadowed in the Treaty convinced her that there was little to hope for from them. It should have been foreseen that a wave of revolt against her sufferings and of reliance upon her own resources would sweep over her. But fantastic and horrible as have been some of its effects, and threatening as must be the situation which it creates, we can hardly believe it possible that so crude a relapse into ideas and practices wholly inconsistent with the present state of civilization can survive when the calamities that produced it have been surmounted. The days of national and racial segregation have so plainly passed away: art, science, finance, industry, commerce, indeed all human interests save the political, are so rapidly becoming international and world-wide that the attempt to contract out of the comity of peoples, though fraught with grave peril, is opposed to the whole trend of human progress, and can only succeed if it smashes all that we now mean by civilization.

The fundamental question of the value of racial purity on which the new Aryanism has pronounced so vigorously is indeed one of the major problems of sociology. We ought to expect from scientific investigation some guidance on two aspects of it at present obscure. Is the general effect of inter-racial marriages eugenic or dysgenic? There is a prejudice against the half-caste; and this at present puts him at a disadvantage. But there seems no positive evidence that the mingling of racial stocks necessarily produces an inferior type. Is there any biological justification for the widespread psychic revulsion against members of other races which produces the "colour bar?" The prejudice may be solely due to comparatively superficial causes, cultural and economic rather than physical: it is certainly accentuated where there is room for fear or rivalry. But here again fuller knowledge is required before we can speak with confidence.

Whatever the final decision, whether the future will maintain or gradually abandon racial segregation, there can be no doubt of the necessity for co-operation. The human family may organize itself in different households, allotting to each its appropriate share of the earth's surface, or it may become interfused and cosmopolitan. In either case it cannot remain in water-tight compartments, each household a self-sufficient unit, armed against its neighbours and owing no allegiance except to its own interests. That phase of development has served its turn. To replace it will take the best of human effort, and may well involve acute tension and many set-backs. But it is a cause of paramount importance; and one to which the Christian is specially committed.

For what the invention of the railway and still more of the bicycle has done for the life of cities and villages, is now being done by broadcasting and aeroplanes for continents and nations. Distance for the sociologist is measurable not by the absolute test of mileage or in the old terms of mountains and seas, but by the relative and variable standards of ease and speed of communication. The European capitals are now far closer together than were London and Edinburgh in the eighteenth century. It is now easier to cross the Atlantic than it was then to cross the Channel, and Japan is nearer than was Norway. Where one man did the grand tour, hundreds are going round the world.

With the difficulties, social, economic, and political, that this revolution in human relationships involves, the statesman is already beginning to be concerned. Neither State nor Church has yet seriously considered the most serious of them—the problem of adjusting population to resources which becomes acute when the natural checks, war, famine, and disease, are removed. But as no one would advocate the starving or infection of overcrowded areas, so to encourage or permit war for the destruction of cannon-fodder ought to be an intolerable solution of the difficulty. Human resources are in fact increasing at least in proportion to the scale and complexity of human problems. To have recourse to obsolete methods for dealing with fresh perplexities is to sin against humanity and against the purpose and development of creation.

It is in fact rather in the moral and spiritual than in the physical and biological spheres that our present weakness is most evident. National and racial differences are emphasized and made acute by the lack of any clear agreement as to the values and standards of the good life and of any strong and unifying incentive to attain it. At present civilization is becoming superficially uniform. Despite the efforts to preserve languages and local customs, Helsingfors and Naples, London, Cairo, Bombay and Buenos Aires, are very much alike: the daily paper and the motor-bus, the apartment-house and the petrol tin, are universal and symbolic. In fifty years all the apparatus of life may well have become standardized and everywhere familiar. But in the use to which it is put, in the aims and ideals which control it, there is still no fundamental agreement. While men of serious outlook differ radically as to whether this world is a place to be enjoyed or shunned or redeemed, and life in it the one reality or an obsessing illusion or a school of souls, there would seem little prospect of any lasting human co-operation. At present when men are bewildered about matters of principle and inclined to suppose that theory waits upon practice, the perils of such disagreements may be ignored: indeed, there are some who argue that men should agree about their culture and differ about their religion. But in fact it is the basal convictions that ultimately determine conduct both in individuals and races. "In things essential unity; in things non-essential diversity" is surely the only condition of "in all things charity": and the essentials are moral and spiritual. All of which is equivalent to saying that if we are to build the house of humanity which some call the City of God there must be agreement about ground plan and architecture before we can profitably settle questions of material and decoration.

Here then is reinforcement for our plea that it is to the task of moral and religious education, of evangelism in the true sense, that we are called to devote ourselves. No reasonable person wishes to see mankind regimented into a flat and monotonous uniformity. Few can be so content with European civilization as to desire to Westernize the world. But it is plain that scientific training has proved a solvent of the ideas and beliefs of non-Christian peoples, and that the religion of Christ has alone shown itself capable of universal acceptance. The old notion that the chief effect of Christian missions was to impose knickerbockers and nightshirts upon native populations, if it ever had any truth, has long since been refuted. Christian Churches in Asia and Africa are now showing a singular power of developing their common faith along lines suited to their traditions and temperaments, and in so doing are already helping to disclose fresh aspects of its meaning, to sift the authentic gospel from its European accretions, and to enlarge our appreciation of the measure of the fulness of the stature of Christ. Indeed, St. Paul's vision of the one body, animated by the one Spirit but displaying a rich variety of function in its several members—the vision which so powerfully influenced the social movements of last century in Britain—is now assuming a new and world-wide significance. A common faith that transcends the barriers of race and class and sex is essential as the foundation of a world-wide commonwealth.

In the early years of the Church's history that conviction forced itself upon the ancient Empire. Whatever we may think of the sincerity or of the effects of the conversion of Constantine, no one who has studied his career can question his political sagacity. He was in fact one of the most remarkable statesmen of history. Winning his way to a throne which had for more than a century been fatally insecure and which even the genius of Diocletian had failed to establish, Constantine came to the conclusion that the only power on earth capable of giving cohesion and stability to the realm was the Christian Church. With that end he took it into favour, laboured to strengthen its unity, and strove to make it the integrative influence in his dominions. By so doing he postponed the collapse of the civil power for a century; and when it fell under economic and military pressure the Church remained as the

THE CHRISTIAN ALTERNATIVE TO WAR

sole survivor of the wreck. That is not an accident. It should encourage us to undertake our task of world unification confident that we have been given the essential instrument for its accomplishment.

V

We would urge therefore that in the service of the Prince of Peace those who enlist can find a moral equivalent and a satisfying alternative for war. A Peace Army, whatever we may think of the proposals recently made for its creation, is a necessity. But it already exists, and its name is the Church of Jesus Christ.

To say so is to invite the protest with which my Liverpool business man concluded our discussion on disarmament. How can the Church serve as an advocate of peace when it is not only "by schisms rent asunder, by heresies distrest," but in dealing with its divisions has displayed a ferocity so virulent as to set the *odium theologicum* in a category by itself? How can Christians urge the necessity of world unity or expect statesmen to behave generously when hardly any of them seem to care for the reunion of Christendom and when their leaders, even if they desired to be generous, dare not face the outbreak of protest from their followers? Can anyone imagine that an institution whose past is blackened with records of persecution has outgrown that past when it tolerates in its representative journals a bitterness of calumny and misrepresentation which no decent secular paper would dream of allowing? Such questions might be multiplied almost indefinitely.

That the difficulties are enormous anyone who has had experience in matters ecclesiastical or who has a wholesome knowledge of his own weaknesses will not be likely to dispute. To catalogue them once more would be disheartening and unprofitable. Yet if our contention is sound that in such a venture there is a moral equivalent for war, then such difficulties, however vast, are a necessary condition and incentive. It is the magnitude of the effort which makes it worthy of support.

Indeed, in these last years it has become increasingly plain that only if the imagination of mankind were fired and its energies enlisted in a task of superhuman greatness was there any prospect of recovery from depression and inertia. There is, as the war demonstrated, an almost limitless reserve of power latent in human beings. Too often it is frittered away in the conflict between contrasted desires and between desire and performance. Given a sufficient cause it might be released from wastage and made available for service. At least the attempt should be undertaken. If the older and more traditionalist Churches are not ready to move, we should look to groups within them or to the bodies which form the Peace Movement to take the initiative. To appeal to younger men and women to give their lives to the service of reconciliation, to provide funds to enable them to do so,

THE CHRISTIAN ALTERNATIVE TO WAR

and to send them out to the areas where the rule of military power is still unquestioned and at present irreplaceable would be to take a first step towards putting into practice the Christian obligation.

In these days there are very many who desire to give their lives to the service of Christ and the promotion of peace and world brotherhood, but who are unable to accept the traditional types of missionary effort. A book like the recent American volume *Re-thinking Missions* gives abundant evidence of their point of view. Even those of us who dissent most strongly from the proposals to change the character of existing missions or to eliminate the doctrinal and institutional elements from evangelism should recognize that the wish to serve is not confined to those whose chief purpose is conversion, and that the Christian ministry of reconciliation must include a wide range of activities. The objective of the evangelist is after all not merely to add new members to his Church or congregation, but to bring all mankind in all its relationships into conformity with the will of God as this is revealed in Christ. In so doing he can claim as his colleagues all those who labour that men "may have life and have it more abundantly." It is only as the Church learns to welcome all those who are thus led by the Spirit of God into works of love and joy and peace as sons of God and members in the body of Christ that it will escape the ecclesiastical prepossessions and sectarian controversies which so often make Christians despair and non-Christians blaspheme.

Such generosity of temper towards those who, while working for peace and human welfare, are not prepared to accept what is for us the inevitable Christian policy is surely in accordance alike with the example of Christ and with the lessons of history. To combine an uncompromising discipleship with a sensitive regard for the difficulties of working out our convictions in practice demands the ability to speak the truth in love; and this, alas, is rare. If realism often degenerates into opportunism and worldly wisdom, idealism is equally liable to become narrow, arrogant, and impracticable. The records of the Peace Societies have not been free from the exclusiveness and heresy-hunting which have disfigured the history of the Church. If we believe in love not force as the ultimate power, then we shall not advance our cause by bitterness or the refusal to sympathize with those who differ from us as to the steps by which its rule is to be advanced. To welcome the efforts of all men and women of good will and to do nothing to obstruct the achievement of results which make for peace even if they fall short of our desires would seem to be not less part of our duty than is loyalty to our own vision. There is need for guidance in relation not only to our own decisions but to our attitude towards others. The question of the character and use of Sanctions will serve as an example. While refusing to submit our own consciences to the dictates of political common sense or to make the Church an appendage of the League of Nations, it ought surely to be possible for Christians to acquiesce in the internationalizing of armed force while advocating and developing another way of reconciliation. It has been the purpose of these lectures not to criticize other programmes of immediate action, but to urge upon the Church its own special and positive duty.

For indeed, whatever may have been the case in the past, we have now come to the point at which armed force must somehow be superseded, if we are not to lose our opportunity and relapse into barbarism. Christ by His death revealed that there was another and a more effective way of dealing with enemies; recent events have demonstrated once more the truth both of His warnings and of His example. The Churches have denounced war as inconsistent with His teaching: the Nations have solemnly outlawed it. Surely there are among us men and women sufficiently adventurous, sufficiently Christian, to take up the ministry of reconciliation, to exercise it wherever the outlook is most dangerous, and to convince the world that the power of the Spirit is stronger than the arms of the flesh and that in these days warfare is as obsolete and as intolerable as slavery. The times are admittedly critical: at such a crisis the Christian should have no excuse for halting between two opinions: "if the Lord be God, follow Him."

INDEX

Adam, A. I., 149
Aggressiveness, instinct of, 77
Allen, T., 149
Archbishops' Recruiting Campaign, 53
Articles of Religion, 31

Barnes, Bishop E. W., 129
Barth, K., 96–100
British Israel, 91
Brooke, R. C., 43
Brunner, H. E., 104
Buchman, F., 72

Cadoux, C. J., 31, 106
Cambrai, battle of, 135
Catholic Moral theology, 113; saintliness, 121.
Chesterton, G. K., 119
Childers, Erskine, 60
Christ and Peace Campaign, 23; or Caesar, 88
C.O.P.E.C. (Conference on Christian Politics, Economics and Citizenship), 22, 24, 34
Constantine, 107, 178

Double standard in ethics, 117
Drinkwater, J., 68

Evangelism as alternative to war, 177
Evolution and war, 128–42

Fox, G., 98
Free Churches and pacifism, 64

Gandhi, 161
Gas-attacks, 45–8
German theology and social problems, 98
Gray, A. H., 24

Headlam, Bishop A. C., 27
Hingston, R. W. G., 145
Huxley, T. H., 126

Idealism and realism, 109–13
Inspiration not automatic, 74

Jerusalem, I.M. Council at, 94
Johnston, J. L., 149

Killing in war, 81, 157
Kingsley, C., 165
Klausner, J., 55

Lambeth Appeal, 21; Conference resolution, 23, 119
League of Nations Union, 23
Liberal Protestantism, 97
Life and Work Conference, 98
Loch, C. S., 53
Logos-doctrine, 147

Maurice, J. F. D., 98
Montague, C. E., 66
Morgan, C. Lloyd, 169

Nazi movement, 25, 173
New Testament on War, 125–6
Nichols, B., 40, 42, 45
Niebuhr, R., 94, 171

No More War Movement, 23
North-West Frontier, 152

Oman, J., 98
Orchard, W. E., 119

Pacifism in 1914, 63
Palestine, 152
Peace Army, 24, 179
Police action and war, 156–8
Prayer and passivity, 72–4
Psychological warfare, 145

Romance and Christianity, 143, 169
Royden, M., 24

Sheppard, H. R. L., 24
Sherriff, R. C., 41, 143
Sorley, C. H., 149
State as non-moral, 93–5
Studdert-Kennedy, G. A., 118

Thomas Aquinas, 119

Uganda, 161
Unamuno, M., 171

Versailles, Treaty of, 22, 173

Wallas, Graham, 21
Wilberforce, W., and slavery, 52
Worship and guidance, 84–7

For Product Safety Concerns and Information please contact our EU representative GPSR@taylorandfrancis.com
Taylor & Francis Verlag GmbH, Kaufingerstraße 24, 80331 München, Germany

www.ingramcontent.com/pod-product-compliance
Lightning Source LLC
Chambersburg PA
CBHW050637300426
44112CB00012B/1840